THROUGH NAKED BRANCHES

THE LOCKERT LIBRARY OF POETRY IN TRANSLATION

For other titles in the Lockert Library
see page 148

Through Naked Branches

Selected Poems of
Tarjei Vesaas

TRANSLATED AND
EDITED BY

Roger Greenwald

PRINCETON UNIVERSITY PRESS

Published by Princeton University Press, 41 William Street, Princeton, New Jersey 08540
In the United Kingdom: Princeton University Press, Chichester, West Sussex
All Rights Reserved

This translation won the 1996 American-Scandinavian Foundation Translation Prize
Some of the translations have appeared in *WRIT Magazine, Scandinavian Review,
Pequod,* and *The Norseman,* often in slightly different form

Translation of this book was supported in part by an Alice and Corrin Strong Fund
Grant from the American-Scandinavian Foundation, and by a grant from
Norwegian Literature Abroad. Work on the Introduction was supported in part
by a grant from Norway's Royal Ministry of Foreign Affairs (through the
Association for the Advancement of Scandinavian Studies in Canada).

Library of Congress Cataloging-in-Publication Data
Vesaas, Tarjei, 1897–1970.
[Poems. English & Norwegian. Selections]
Through naked branches: selected poems of Tarjei Vesaas /
translated and edited by Roger Greenwald.
p.   cm.   —(Lockert library of poetry in translation)
Poems in both English and Norwegian.
Includes index.
ISBN 0-691-00896-5 (alk. paper).   —ISBN 0-691-00897-3 (alk. paper)
1. Vesaas, Tarjei, 1897–1970 Translations into English.
I. Greenwald, Roger. II. Title. III. Series.
PT 9088.V6T47   2000   839.8'2172—dc21

This book has been composed in Dante

http://pup.princeton.edu

Printed in the United States of America

1 3 5 7 9 10 8 6 4 2

The Lockert Library of Poetry in Translation is supported by a bequest from
Charles Lacy Lockert (1888–1974)

*This translation is dedicated to
Drs. Ragnhild and Mykola Radejko
in appreciation of their hospitality
and their friendship.*

CONTENTS

ACKNOWLEDGMENTS

I am deeply indebted to Halldis Moren Vesaas for her assistance in matters of interpretation and in correcting occasional errors in the published Norwegian texts, for her encouragement and concern, and for her great patience. I am sorry that she did not live to see this book published. I thank Guri Vesaas and Olav Vesaas for their continued support.

These translations would have been much poorer without the generous help of Paal-Helge Haugen, who went over them in detail against the originals. I am grateful to have had the benefit, too, of critical comment on the English texts from several friends: Luigi M. Bianchi, Bjørnar Hassel, Inger Haug, and Richard Lush.

The Introduction I struggled with for many years. In the course of those years I drew inspiration from conversations with more people than I could name here. But I would like to add a special note of thanks to those who read long draft versions and offered me their criticisms and suggestions: Peter Anson, Luigi M. Bianchi, Torben Brostrøm, Michael Dixon, Peter Harries-Jones, Inger Haug, Paal-Helge Haugen, Richard Lush, Tricia Postle, and Lasse Tømte. Alf Magne Heskja kindly loaned me his copy of Arne Næss's seminal book on ecology and also gave me free access to his computer and printer.

I thank Steinar Gimnes for sending me copies of his articles; Per Buvik for extending the hospitality of the Department of Comparative Literature at the University of Bergen; and Hans Morten Kind of that university's High Technology Center for friendly technical assistance. As ever, I am grateful for the sympathetic help, far beyond the call of duty, offered by Eva Lie-Nielsen of Gyldendal Norsk Forlag.

R. G.
May 1998

INTRODUCTION

For a Norwegian reader and for any literate Scandinavian, the name Tarjei Vesaas conjures up an entire ethos. Many English-speaking readers may enter that ethos with relative ease, but if they attempt to analyze, discuss, or even just think about the work, they will face greater challenges than they might expect in dealing with poetry from a culture apparently similar to their own. For example, trying to account for the freshness of a poem like the opening one in Vesaas's first book of poetry, "Snow and Spruce Forest," which has "home" in its first line and "hearts" in its last, challenges the reader to confront the issue of modernity and received ideas about its relation to the urban. Likewise, acknowledging Vesaas's uses of animation and personification for the depth they yield, rather than seeing them as forms of literary naiveté or as anachronisms, as throwbacks to the Romantics, requires us to reconceive the philosophical framework in which we understand the relation of humans to nature. After a brief biographical outline, I will develop some of the critical concepts and vocabulary I think are needed to grapple with these issues.

Tarjei Vesaas was born in 1897 near the town of Vinje in Telemark, on the Vesaas farm, which his family had worked for nine generations. As the eldest son, he was expected by long tradition to take over the farm. But his talent was to decree otherwise. He published his first novel in 1923, his second in 1924, his third, and a play as well, in 1925. A travel grant that year took him first to Sweden and Denmark, then to Germany, Italy, and France. An award in 1927 enabled him to stay abroad for two years; on this journey he toured or lived in Munich, Paris, London, Cologne, Vienna, and other cities. With the help of another travel grant, in 1931 he visited the poet Halldis Moren where she was working in Switzerland; they married in 1934 and settled on the farm Midtbø, a stone's throw from the Vesaas farm. Here he lived and worked until his death in 1970. The Vesaases raised two children.

By the end of 1934, Vesaas had published ten novels, two plays, and a collection of short stories. From 1935 to the occupation of Norway by Nazi Germany in 1940, he published three more novels and a second volume of stories. He kept writing during the occupation, but could not publish the work until after the country was liberated.

In 1946, in his late forties and well established as a major writer of fiction, Vesaas published his first volume of poems (he had written verse sporadically for many years, but had published only a few pieces in periodicals). He was to issue five such volumes during his lifetime; a sixth—by general consensus the strongest collection—would appear posthumously in 1970. But he by no means "went over" to poetry: from 1935 to 1970 he published ten novels (among them several of his acknowledged masterpieces), two volumes of stories, and a play. The collection of stories called *Vindane* [The Winds] (1952) won the Venice Prize; the novel *Is-slottet* (*The Ice Palace*) (1963) earned him the Nordic Council Prize. His fiction was translated—and continues to be translated—into many languages; eight novels have appeared in English. His place as one of the giants of Scandinavian fiction in this century is secure.

It was inevitable in a career like Vesaas's that the fiction would overshadow the poetry (the careers of Hardy and Lawrence offer similar examples). Yet I would argue that Vesaas's best poems are in a class with those of Rolf Jacobsen (1907–94) and Olav H. Hauge (1907–94), who are widely recognized as the greatest Norwegian poets of the modern period.

Vesaas's fiction and his poetry are closely related. Especially in his writing in the postwar period, the reader can not only feel the presence of the same sensibility behind the work in the two genres, but can recognize the voice, and with some care can derive from the fiction a notion of Vesaas's symbolic vocabulary that may be useful in grasping the range of connotations in the usually compact poems. I cannot hope to supply the background of Vesaas's artistic world here; to anyone who wishes to explore it I recommend the novel *Fuglane* (*The Birds*) (1957). (The quotations gathered in the appendix I offer not for the facts they may yield, but for whatever "feel" of Tarjei Vesaas may survive in the translation.)

Vesaas has been described as a realist, a symbolist, a realist symbolist, a Romantic, a modernist, and a modernist primitivist; naturalist and expressionist elements have been traced in his works. Granted, he wrote a great many books over a long period, and some of them work very differently from others. But many critics have themselves been dissatisfied with their tools—both with their "ism's" and with many of the ideas they have tried to apply to Vesaas. The Danish critic Torben Brostrøm, though his essays on Vesaas are models of insight and eloquence, remarks that anyone who sets out to write about Vesaas and is not excessively cynical will feel "that he is bound to tear apart things that belong together...."[1]

Such insistence on the difficulty of paraphrasing Vesaas or of describing discursively what lies at the core of his art points, I think, to certain qualities of Vesaas's work, and to the inadequacy for dealing with them of some of our customary critical approaches. We need a framework in which the poetry can be discussed and appreciated without the nagging sense that the work and the critical terms are at odds with each other. I will propose two key parts of such a framework.

My first proposition is that Vesaas is not primarily a visual poet. I put this negatively (to begin with) for two reasons: because a deliberate effort is needed to overcome both the general domination of our habits of thought by the visual sense and the overwhelmingly visual orientation of most modern poetry, and with it of most criticism; and because even a reader thoroughly familiar with Vesaas's poetry may assume—under the sway of the habits just mentioned, and perhaps from experience of much other Scandinavian poetry—that his poems work mainly through their visual imagery. Although there are of course visual descriptions, they are rarely detailed, and even when they are, they seldom drive the powerful moments in the poems (for an exception, see "Dead Lake"—but note the key adjective, "mute"). In fact, Vesaas sometimes insists explicitly on the limitations or shortcomings of visual perception ("Snow and Spruce Forest," "The Smell of Spring").

Vesaas has roots in an oral tradition. That tradition includes not only oral narrative, but also oral poetry. In a survey of Vesaas's poetry published in 1964, Yngvil Molaug Stang remarks that whenever Vesaas writes in conventional forms (and he did so, though with decreasing frequency, throughout his career), "the ring of the folk song is unmistakable." This is immediately evident to a Norwegian reader—and for the most part inaudible in my translations of such poems. But Stang goes on to record two less common perceptions: that even after Vesaas has developed a concise, concentrated poetic style, "the old art forms of Telemark [i.e., sung poems, including mythic, epic and ballad forms] resonate in the modern instrument"; and further, that "there is a music from the *Edda* in these poetic forms that can recall, in its tight rhythm, the [skaldic]

[1] Torben Brostrøm, "Frigørelsens veje," in *Tarjei Vesaas*, ed. Jan Erik Vold (Oslo: Kulturutvalget i Det Norske Studentersamfund, 1964), 184. All translations of quoted material are my own unless otherwise indicated.

fornyrdislag."[2] (The reader in English will, I hope, be able to detect such rhythm in "Snow and Spruce Forest," "The Boat on Land," "Through Naked Branches," and "The Mountain That Wept.") These connections to oral tradition have been little remarked, but taken together with what we may regard as Vesaas's temperamental affinity for the aural, they have important consequences for how we conceive of his sensibility, his poetry, and the poetry's relation to the mainstream of modernism.

"For better or worse," writes Denis Donoghue, "the high poetry of this century . . . the poetry we agree to call 'modern' . . . has proceeded on Symbolist lines":

> [I]t is characteristic of Symbolism to identify Imagination with Vision. . . . The Symbolist poet assumes that meaning is available as a visual pattern, often a pattern imposed by the imagination. This accounts for our sluggishness in coming to terms with poets who live by a different allegiance; as Whitman's allegiance . . . is contact, and Yeats's is action.[3]

Vesaas's allegiance in his poetry, I would argue, is to *hearing*. Vesaas's most nightmarish poem, "In Thrall," is one in which the speaker is deprived of his hearing: his ears simply fall off. Yet still he attends to what *would* be audible if he could hear: "In my peculiar silence I understood that the air was boiling / with sound." Time and again, the crucial moments in Vesaas's poems are those in which something is heard: a call ("March 1945," "The Loons Head North," "The Boat," "Sun-corner"); a voice, whether outer or inner ("A Word in the Fall"; "Outside the Wind Whispers"); the sounds of snow or ice, wind or water, leaves or birds, hauled timber or thunder; and silences—demanding silences ("The Horse"), inarticulate silences ("A Word in the Fall," "Shy Word"), tired, calm, fulfilled, loving, confusing, ominous, terrifying silences. (Note that in "The Glass Wall," the I and the you can see each other; the essential connection that is blocked is that of sound/voice/speech.) The poet listens, others listen, and sometimes the surroundings seem to listen as well.

---

[2] Yngvil Molaug Stang, "Lyrikken," in *Ei bok om Tarjei Vesaas*, ed. Leif Mæhle (Oslo: Det Norske Samlaget, 1964), 226. Also see 235–36, 269–70.

[3] Denis Donoghue, *The Ordinary Universe* (1968, rpt. New York: Ecco, 1987), 125. Although I have chosen to focus on the modern literary arena, it is worth noting that Coleridge objected to the "tyranny of the eye" and its constraint of abstract thought, and that many philosophers and critics have since explored (and objected to) the dominance of the visual in Western culture.

The terror comes when the silence is empty: because the poet has no answer ("The Horse") or because he can detect only coldness, death, the void ("Dead Lake").

Vesaas's primary allegiance to the oral/aural rather than the visual puts his work outside, and in some ways at odds with, the visually oriented movement dominant in modern poetry. Torben Brostrøm found something unique when he first read Vesaas:

> I felt that I saw something in the novels and found something in concentrated form in his poems that did not resemble Norwegian poetry or anything else.
> . . . .
> He wasn't very talkative, rather a listener. It wasn't a brooding silence he had about him, but a field of sensitivity and slow readiness. A dreaming mixture of inner and outer worlds. . . .
>
> I would nonetheless call it a modern condition. Not common. In no way related to fashion. But modern in the sense of "productive fission." A desperation transformed into creation, with balance as the result.[4]

It is a mark of Vesaas's modernity that his listening does not necessarily discern meaning; and a mark of his difference that it does not discern only an echoing abyss either. In Vesaas the listener stands in a relation of dynamic tension to what he listens to, which involves something other than his own voice. There is an order beyond what derives from the self, but it is often inscrutable and angst-inducing: "No one knows the levels / at the bottom of Lake Angst" ("Endlessly Rowing"). Literal acts of hearing in Vesaas can be taken to carry with them a bodily impression, a sensory reminder, of an "inner hearing" that corresponds to the type of faculty we more commonly meet as "inner sight."

If Vesaas's allegiance to hearing supplies much of the crucial imagery of his poems, and even some of their narrative matter, it also exerts a controlling influence on their form. The periods, line breaks and stanza breaks often create pauses that suggest the rhythm of the listening process which has yielded the knowledge being conveyed (whether the listening attends to sounds, impressions, or the poet's own thoughts). Consider a stanza from "A Word in the Fall" (the translation has eliminated one line break):

[4] Torben Brostrøm, "Det umættelige mørke," café Existens, No. 39/40 (1989), 6. I have reservations about the adjective "dreaming," as I will explain later.

> We went to the earth.
> To everyone's earth.
> We were shy of calling her
> what she was for us.

The pause after the first line enacts the moment of realization that the earth stands in a close relation to the "we" and that the relation is the same for everyone. The second line restates, refines; but for the moment, "everyone's" suggests the earth is ours, we possess it. In the next pause, "we" realize that the earth possesses us as much as we possess it (as the phrase "our mother" indicates both the mother we have and the mother who has us); but this remains unstated, can be deduced only at the end of the stanza. The next line break preserved in the translation enacts the shy hesitation to give the relation a name; and indeed, when the last line comes, it avoids naming, so that the pause before it is retroactively filled with a brief search for the last line's tactful dodge.

The meanings emerge literally between the lines, where the pauses demand an attentiveness from the reader to match the poet's own. A glance at the stanza breaks in this poem will show that they work in a similar fashion: at each break the poet seems to reflect on the previous stanza, which is echoed in the first line of the next one; he then proceeds to a greater depth of perception, which arrives in the second line (second or third in the original).

Of course there are also lyrical pieces in which the voice flows continuously, the thoughts and feelings coming without gaps. But pauses or a lack of them are not the only formal features that express Vesaas's allegiance to hearing. His sensitivity to the rhythms of speech, of breath, and of bodily movement—together with a mastery of the sonic resources of his language—produces poems whose pace, phrasing and sound patterns embody the "feel" of the experiences they deal with. In "Snow and Spruce Forest," for example, the three parallel lines in the next-to-last stanza convey the rhythm of walking up a slope through snow to approach and touch a tree; while the refrain "the whole, whole time" ("heile heile tida") makes us enact the huffing of breath into the cold air.

To say this is perhaps to say no more than that Vesaas's allegiance as _craftsman_ was also to hearing—that we are meant not only to attend to the "voices" he listened to, but to hear the poems themselves, whether we read silently or aloud—to feel them "mixed into our own breath." Yet given the direction much modern poetry has taken (in Norway as elsewhere), the point seems worth making. In poetry that is to be heard, I would distinguish, roughly, two poles, speech and song, each of which, if written well, has its own music. (Usually Vesaas speaks rather than sings, and moreover speaks in a low voice: the poet Tor Ulven notes that "strangely enough, even italicized lines that end in exclamation points sound muted in Vesaas."[5]) But more to the point here, it has become necessary to distinguish between poetry that is to be heard and poetry that is merely to be seen. I do not refer to the difference between the truly oral poetry of older cultures and the written poetry that has largely supplanted it, but to the difference within the realm of written poetry between the kind that aims at creating some sort of voice and the kind that aspires to the condition of mime.[6]

It is not paradoxical, but logical, that a poet who writes for the ear can produce powerful silences. The soft voice gives rise to silence around it, in us who attend to it; the thought process embodied in the poems gives rise to silence between the lines; the deliberate pace gives rise to silence between phrases.

My second proposition is that Vesaas's special relation to nature, the key (as many have recognized) to his whole way of writing, is of a kind that we can understand *critically* only if we will rethink some of our basic models of mind and world. That Vesaas's poetry can be understood *intuitively* without such rethinking is an index of its power; that it demands such rethinking of the critic is an index of its importance. The difficulty is that our habitual concepts and terms often contain precisely the premises we will need to abandon or revise.

The first impulse of an English-speaking reader may be to regard Vesaas as a rural/regional writer. This would be inadequate on two counts. First, Vesaas's travels and his access to contemporary literature from England and the Continent meant that he was in no way isolated from the literary developments of his day. Second, and more important, the "map" implicit in our notion of regional writers does not apply to Norway, or at least not to Norway as it was during Vesaas's lifetime. In the early part of the twentieth century, eighty percent of the population

[5] Tor Ulven, "Hjem til det ukjente," *café Existens*, No. 39/40 (1989), 78.

[6] Some "silent" poets are simply oblivious to the entire dimension of sound and thus, in a sense, to silence itself. Others write as they do from a profound respect for silence and a reluctance to disturb it.

lived in the countryside, there was a strong literary tradition outside the cities, and the description and codification of the nonurban dialects by nineteenth-century linguists working under the sway of growing nationalist feeling had lent ever greater weight and prestige to that tradition.[7]

Literate Norway was to be found in the country as well as in the cities. And if a writer can be truly modern without being urban, his work demands that we reconsider at least one of our customary criteria for modernity.[8] The Danish writer Martin A. Hansen suggests that "the modern [Norwegian] writer finds something new in the village, not the singular, but the universal." Surrounded by hills and forests, he nonetheless finds a perch that offers the broadest sort of perspective.[9]

Having put aside at least our initial assumptions about the rural, we are at once faced with a larger challenge. It is difficult for English-speaking readers, when confronted with poetry in which nature plays any sort of central role, to avoid perceiving that poetry with reference to the attitudes we are familiar with from the work of the English Romantics. In our everyday way of thinking we share with the Romantics a conception of nature as material, external, and "inanimate" (without anima, or spirit—even if we posit no other source for spirit than ourselves). But there is a difference: the Romantics had enough direct, intimate contact with nature to *sense*, at rare moments, a participation or interplay between humans and nature. Most modern urban dwellers do not have much direct, intimate contact with nature, and therefore have little reason to doubt their conceptual framework. Those who no longer have access to the direct experience of unitary meanings have *conscious* experi-

[7] Vesaas wrote in Nynorsk, one of Norway's two official languages or written norms. (Put simply, Nynorsk covers the nonurban dialects, Bokmål the urban ones.) For most of the period when Vesaas was publishing, fierce debates raged in Norway about the cultural significance and relative merits of the two written norms, their suitability for various genres, their places in the school curriculum and the media, and their future. Much literary criticism was colored by the views of the critics on language issues, so it can be difficult to tease apart the various sources of energy that fueled critical responses to the use of the rural or of nature in the books of that time. I will have occasion to focus on some Norwegian critics' attitudes toward the use of nature in modern Norwegian writing, but it is beyond the scope of this essay to address the role of linguistic factors in shaping those attitudes. (I am grateful to Lasse Tømte for calling my attention to this issue.)

[8] See, e.g., M. L. Rosenthal's remarks about Robert Frost in *The Modern Poets* (New York: Oxford University Press, 1960, rpt. 1965), 110.

[9] Hansen, "Fortælleren fra Vinje," in *Midsommerkrans* (Copenhagen: Gyldendal, 1956), 125.

ence of such meanings mainly in art—where they will accept the simultaneity of literal and symbolic import because art is sponsored by human intention. (Metaphor *imitates* unitary meanings, but in fact its uniting of outer and inner import depends on their having been separate first.)[10]

I would propose that some modern writers have managed to experience the world directly as a complex field of relations, and have managed to embody knowledge of that experience in their work, aided by our continued ability to apprehend a kind of unified meaning in art. But it is difficult for us to see that this is what they have done, for as soon as their work involves nature in any way, we are apt to see intimations of interplay between humans and nature as a throwback, and to regard these writers as "Romantic"—or worse, as pretending to indulge in an experience that the Romantics, even as they longed for it, felt was impossible, or was nearly so and was fast becoming entirely so. (There are of course writers who do pretend in this way, and we are right to find their work naive, or inauthentic, or strained—as we find much "nature writing" of the inspirational, "poetic" sort, unless it is frankly religious.)

As extraordinary as it may sound, I think the degree of intimacy with nature that the great English Romantics felt they achieved only rarely is for Vesaas a *starting point*. But as long as we see nature mechanically, no amount of formulation and reformulation about modern writers who have a more sophisticated dealing with nature will manage to say much about this essential aspect of their work. They will inevitably emerge as atavistic. If we sense nonetheless that they are genuinely modern, we will be left merely asserting this, and insisting there is "something" else in their work that cannot be described.

For example, in his book on William Carlos Williams, James E. B. Breslin remarks that Williams, "like so many of the modernist generation, [is] a poet whose anti-Romanticism is a cover for his latent Romanticism." Breslin states his reason for this characterization as follows:

[A] sacred principle clearly resides at the center of Williams's poetics. He gives it many different names . . . because no name, no words, can ever fully capture this elusive, hidden "presence." Williams stresses its manifestation in physicality—the body or the earth—and he does not

[10] See Owen Barfield, *Saving the Appearances: A Study in Idolatry* (New York: Harcourt Brace Jovanovich, 1965), 121; and *Poetic Diction*, 3rd ed. (Middletown, CT: Wesleyan University Press, 1973), 77–82.

imagine it as existing separately from matter[,] and so it is hard to call it transcendent. Yet this principle is eternal, universal . . . and sacred, and so it is hard not to call it transcendent.[11]

In its way, this is, I think, both perceptive and accurate. Yet, when we find ourselves saying a poet is anti-Romantic but in fact Romantic, and that an essential principle in his work is not transcendent, but transcendent nonetheless, then we may wonder whether our terms are not simply inadequate, inappropriate to the case at hand. It may be, of course, that certain texts embody a paradox that only paradoxical formulations can suggest. But it may also be that the texts embody an integral apprehension, and that we need to find critical concepts that can convey their integrity, rather than imply that they must be mixtures (and even contradictory mixtures).

What I have been saying here and what I am leading to have much in common with the following observations, made by George Steiner over twenty years ago. These remarks address the relation of mind to body, but quickly show that they have a wider relevance.

Granted numerous sophistications, it is none the less true that our daily language and routine imaginings do still operate with a rough and ready mind-body dualism. In our unexamined recourse to such polarities as psychic and physical, mental and bodily, innate and environmental, we have scarcely improved very much on the dissociative schemes of Cartesian and idealist philosophy. . . . When we bother to reflect, to consider the evidence, we know, of course, that this crude dualism won't do. The categories are hopelessly indiscriminate; the intermediate zones, the modes of interaction and reciprocal determination, are far too manifold. . . . Wherever we turn . . . [we] find correlative revaluations of the whole model of how the mind and body may fit together. It is by now, surely, an honest commonplace to say that consciousness acts on the environment, that consciousness is, in some sense, the environmental structure, and that the reciprocities between the immaterial and the material are ones of dynamic feedback. Everywhere, the old divorcement of spirit and flesh is yielding to a much more complex metaphor of continuum.[12]

[11]James E. B. Breslin, *William Carlos Williams: An American Artist* (Chicago: University of Chicago Press, 1985), xi, x.

[12]George Steiner, *Nostalgia for the Absolute* (Toronto: Canadian Broadcasting Cor-poration, 1974), 42–43. What Steiner could not have anticipated in 1974 was the way in

There have of course been thinkers in various fields who have developed models based on interaction, but their work has had a much greater popular impact in fields that describe interactions among people (where we are obliged to recognize that there are two or more meaning-generating subjectivities at play) than in fields that describe interactions between people on the one hand and the nonhuman environment on the other. (It will save trouble if I specify here that I do not mean "interact" to imply that the environment "acts" in a sense that indicates volition.)

Even a simple sketch of an interactive model should enable us better to understand both modern texts that make use of nature and the quandaries they have caused for critics. Here it will be helpful to draw on pioneering work on the relations of humans to nature—written, it should come as no surprise, by a Norwegian, the philosopher Arne Næss (widely credited with founding "deep ecology"). I cannot hope even to summarize Næss's main arguments, but a few key points should suffice.

> Among the educated public the dominant [view] today is no doubt that mathematically informed science gives the approximately correct description of the environment as it *is in itself.*[13]

> [But] physicists by no means need to imagine that nature is *really* and *objectively* so very different from the way we experience it. They can rest content, and in fact often do so, with asserting that *on the basis of certain models,* a table or a universe must be described in this or that way. They do not "absolutize." Only the study of methodology can help us understand the function of models of thought in physics and thereby release us from the many futile attempts to distinguish between things and nature in themselves, "an sich," and nature for me, "an mich." It is advantageous to eliminate the distinction itself.[14]

> "Objective descriptions of nature" of the type physics gives us should not

---

which the proliferation of digital computers would affect our metaphors and our thinking, introducing a new model which, if different in certain ways from the nineteenth-century mechanical one, is nonetheless reductionist.

[13] Arne Næss, *Økologi, samfunn og livsstil,* 5th ed. (Oslo: Universitetsforlaget, 1976), 42. The book is densely argued but clearly written. An English version, *Ecology, Community, and Lifestyle,* trans. and revised by David Rothenberg (Cambridge and New York: Cambridge University Press, 1991), is rather heavy going. All quotations here are my translations from the Norwegian. The italics are Næss's in all quotations from his work.

[14] Næss, *Økologi,* 43.

be considered descriptions of *nature*, but descriptions (with the help of models) of certain interdependencies (relations, structures). . . .[15]

In some contexts Næss prefers not to use the term "interaction" at all:

> Organisms must be defined as relational nodes in the total field. "Interaction" between the organism and the environment gives incorrect associations, for the organism *is* interaction—in a certain sense. Organism and environment are not two *things* that are in more or less intimate contact. . . . Organism assumes environment.[16]

> [O]ne moves from description of a thing in an environment to description of a field in which thing and environment can no longer be sharply separated.[17]

One could paraphrase this by saying that relations are internal rather than external. An internal relation is one that is so important that if it ceases to exist, one or both of the "items" that stand in relation to each other can no longer be said to be the same things they were before. (Næss grants that internal relations need not always be reciprocal.)[18]

A crucial implication of this way of thinking is that it is our embeddedness in the field which includes both our surroundings and us that gives rise to both phenomena and their significance. There is no reason to imagine that we "project" order and significance onto an anarchic and passive environment. As Næss concludes: *"To speak of projection into the thing is to invent a complicated model without methodological value."*[19]

This has far-reaching consequences. If a forest is a "something" with properties that, in relation to our nervous system (however modified by culture) gives rise to the phenomenon "forest," then a *gloomy forest* is also a "something" with properties that, in relation to our nervous system (however modified by culture) gives rise to the phenomenon "gloomy forest." One cannot have it both ways and say the forest is "actual" and the gloom only "projected"—that is, that there is a "something" in the world which gives rise to the phenomenon forest, but that there is noth-

---

[15] Næss, *Økologi*, 44–45.

[16] Næss, *Økologi*, 52. See also 77, 293.

[17] Næss, *Økologi*, 55–56.

[18] See Arne Næss, *Self-realization: An Ecological Approach to Being in the World*, the Fourth Keith Roby Memorial Lecture in Community Sciences (Murdoch, Australia: Murdoch University, 1986), 7 (unpaginated).

[19] Næss, *Økologi*, 298.

ing in the world, outside us, that gives rise to the phenomenon gloomy forest. This would be to say, in short, that how we feel in the forest has nothing to do with the forest. I do not mean that "gloominess" inheres in the forest. I mean only that the forest has certain properties that may, in relation to us, give rise to our perception of gloom. That I may experience the forest differently from you, or differently on different days—when, after all, the forest will be altered—does not affect my argument.[20]

> The expression or character of the environment . . . is neither something subjective within man, nor something to be found outside, but an aspect of man's being in the world.[21]

Næss explores this issue at some length, dealing, among other things, with the traditional philosophical division of qualities into primary, secondary, and tertiary (the primary are ascribed to things in themselves, the secondary and tertiary are said to arise within us). He concludes: "Consciousness is not, then, a sort of container where the tertiary qualities reside."[22]

> This is a viewpoint whose effect is to *sever human reality from actual nature*. All the prestige goes to what is at the core of the proper and the orderly, the measurable and scientific, and utterly without smell or colors or light or form: completely inaccessible, speeding spirals of elementary particles. That is the "proper reality." Everything else is romantic concoctions.[23]

In simple terms, "it is unwarranted to believe that how we feel nature to be is not like how nature really is."[24]

The relational model I have outlined here changes our picture of us and our surroundings in a basic way. If one has a nineteenth-century model, from which God has been erased, then finding significance in nature entails reintroducing God. The phenomena must be either dead or animated (inspirited) by God, so they are kept dead. Since God was the

[20] For Næss's slightly different presentation of this argument, see *Self-realization*, 14 (unpag.) and *Økologi*, 46–49, 55–56.

[21] Christian Norberg-Schulz, *Existence, Space and Architecture* (New York: Praeger, 1971), 34.

[22] Næss, *Økologi*, 56.

[23] Næss, *Økologi*, 49.

[24] Næss, *Self-realization*, 14 (unpag.). Owen Barfield also explores this idea in a provocative way. See *Saving the Appearances*, chaps. 1–2.

source of all spirit, spirit was essentially a religious element; though it dwelled in creation, in its essence it was with God, and therefore also ultimately unknowable. If one removes God from the picture, one necessarily removes spirit as well; as it vanishes from the far side of the divide, it withdraws also from its dwelling-places on this side.

The relational model, on the other hand, puts together mankind and the universe in such a way that significance arises from the relation between the two. I think it is fruitful to call the sum of all the properties in us and the world that give rise to such significance "spirit," even though the word threatens to bring with it connotations that such a cautiously restrictive definition seeks to exclude. In this model, significance arises without divine intention; and spirit exists without (necessarily) having a divine source.[25]

If we now turn to Vesaas with our relational model, we will find subtlety and depth where before we might have seen only "traditional" devices. There are several ways in which nature is important in Vesaas's poetry—as in the poetry of many modern Norwegian poets; and there are many ways in which that importance manifests itself. One of the most striking of these, animation, attracts special notice from the English-speaking reader precisely because it has been out of fashion in English poetry for a long time—and indeed, in most European poetry as well. It ranges from assigning lifelike qualities to nonliving entities, through describing animals or things as if they could think and feel as we do, to using some aspect of the human form in a metaphor in which the other element is nonhuman. (Thus I am using "animation" as a generic term to cover "animation" in a narrower sense, "inspiriting," "anthropomorphism," and "personification.")

Modern Norwegian poetry has had a much greater tolerance for ani-

[25] The word "spirit" inevitably causes unease in many people who believe (as I believe) that all phenomena arise from matter, that there is no nonmaterial substance (there are, however, nonmaterial phenomena, such as logical relations). Yet I think the vocabulary we already have for discussing our relation to the universe and our feelings about that relation—largely a vocabulary of spirit—will turn out to be both useful and necessary, just as the vocabulary we had for mental phenomena turned out to be useful and necessary, and will remain so, in spite of any knowledge we now have or may yet gain about the functioning of neurons in our nervous systems. Thus, when I refer to a spiritual dimension of awareness, I do not mean anything occult or otherworldly, but rather an apprehension (which may or may not be accompanied by awe) of the enormous, complex field in which people are points or nodes.

mation than poetry in English has had. One reason for this is probably that Norwegian poets have had a great deal to say about the character of natural phenomena, both for their own sake and for the purpose of expressing symbolically certain perceptions about people. Another reason must be that animation accords not only with many poets' way of thinking about the world, but with their way of being in the world. And we should be prepared to entertain the notion that this way of being may be advanced rather than backward in relation to the nineteenth-century mechanical model. We should not assume, when a Norwegian poet uses metaphors that join the terms of human action to the terms of natural events, that he intends to imply that natural objects "act" as we do, from intention and volition. Nor do I think most Norwegian readers would assume this.

If they are candid with foreigners about their dealings with nature, not only Norwegian writers, but Norwegians in all walks of life are apt to find themselves accused of animism. But what does that accusation (or in the best case, description) really mean? In the case of primitive peoples, if we regard animism as a mere "manner of thinking"—i.e., if we suppose that they knew it was not "literally" true that gods or other active entities inhabited rivers and stones and trees—then we make the mistake of supposing those peoples had the same concept of "literal" that we have. Since modern poets live and work in a culture dominated by science, however, it is easy for us to suppose that for *them* a presentation of nature as animate must surely be only a "manner of speaking." But in fact it reflects a knowledge similar to that of the "primitives"—which is not to say that complexity theory or deep ecology is the same as primitive animism, but that they have in common a notion of the "literal" that is different from the scientific notion. They draw their boundaries otherwise than reductionist materialism does. So a different conceptual framework is part of what is embodied in and expressed by the poets' use of animation. That framework is only "animist" from the point of view of a reductionist, who applies that label to a sort of knowledge that lies outside his own framework; and it is only "transcendental" from the point of view of a narrow rationalist, who likewise applies *that* label to a sort of knowledge that lies outside *his* framework.

As Næss observes,

gestalts bind I and not-I together into a whole. Joy becomes not *my* joy, but *something joyous* that includes the I and something else as interdependent, non-isolable fragments. "The birch laughed / with all birches' bright light laughter . . ." This gestalt is *a creation* which can only partly be split into an I who projects and a birch tree.

The glorification of sober, super-reasonable, "scientific" thinking leads to the ridiculing of such creations. It tears apart the gestalts in the world of immediate experience and in the worlds of culture.[26]

In early poems (see, e.g., "The Loons Head North" and "Between Blue Shadows"), Vesaas may occasionally ascribe an apparently human—or greater than human—sympathy to a part of nature. But in later poems he rarely assigns to natural objects even an image of human action, much less one of human feeling. What he does do is to speak of life forms or man-made objects as having a kind of knowledge or as expressing a kind of message.

> The boats on the sand have drawn together
> as if in a council of elders.
> . . . .
> What they don't know about the wet
> no one knows.
>
> ("The Boats on the Sand")

Most often, Vesaas restricts himself to personification that uses human *form*. Thus, in "The Footprints," Vesaas describes a secluded lakeshore closed off by "scorched" mountains, an arc of sand that bears one person's tracks. The speaker concludes that the person had been waiting for someone who never came. (The theme of anxious anticipation is a common one in Vesaas, and it is typical of what one might call his "triangulating" approach to time in his poems that "The Footprints" begins in the moment soon *after* the footprints were made, then moves to their making in a *before* that never yielded an event!)[27]

> The sand was completely closed off by strange
> mountains.
> . . . .

[26] Næss, *Økologi*, 300. See also 298–99. For a recent debate on post-reductionist science, see *Nature's Imagination: The Frontiers of Scientific Vision*, ed. John Cornwall (Oxford: Oxford University Press, 1995).

[27] See Harald Beyer, "Symbolikken hos Vesaas: spreidde tankar," *Syn og segn* (1947), 267; and Torben Brostrøm, review of *Ver ny, vår draum*, in *Information*, quoted in "Vesaas 'hører græset gro,'" *Norsk tidend*, 27 Oct. 1956, 5.

The trail of your young foot in a frenzy,
your soft steps, in thirst, before you fled.
Your best dream, for no one.
Your golden form, wasted.
. . . .
—while the black cliffs looked on
with streaks down their features
from previous lives.

The original has, literally, "stood over" where I have "looked on," and since the word for "stood" in Norwegian, as in English, can indicate mere position (as in "The dresser stood next to the bed"), the translation here puts rather more personification into the poem than it actually has. The Norwegian nouns in the next line, like English "streaks" and "features," can have both (or either one of) human and nonhuman meanings. One could regard this choice of words as subtly noncommittal (or neutral), or as subtly unifying. But what of "previous lives," then? Since there is nothing in the poem that assigns organic life to the scorched mountains, we have no reason to think this line does so either. The mountains have had "previous lives" in the sense that they have endured through countless periods and cycles. They have also "stood over" previous human lives, as they stand over the one evoked here. To the extent that the streaks may be seen as humanlike traits, they may be regarded not merely as an image the poet uses to describe the mountains, but as an image he supposes would have occurred to the person who waited (and to others who had waited there before). The lines that begin with "Your" take us into that person's thoughts as the poet imagines them. Vesaas begins the poem with a single instance of waiting, imagines it as the turning point in an entire human life (or at least, imagines someone who felt it might be), and ends up using the great age of the mountains to evoke a whole chain of human lives lived out under them—and in interplay with them. This is very far from a naive "projecting" of human attributes onto nature.

A poem by Rolf Jacobsen in which the "personification" works in a similar fashion casts further light on this issue. Jacobsen describes a mountain that has a large

steep brow
without any thoughts in it. It stood here
through Belsen and Hiroshima. It stands here now
as a landmark for your death, your unease,

perhaps your hopes.
So you can go over there and hold onto something
    hard.

. . . .

[A]nd think your thoughts through.
And think for yourself.[28]

What is the point of saying the mountain has a *brow* if one is immediately going to say that it does not think? The answer is right here. The mountain is a steady, enduring thing that helps us to keep our bearings, and to think for ourselves. Its very emptiness of thought is an advantage: no opinions, no propaganda, no noise. It is of course we who make it a landmark, but it must have properties that allow us to do so. "Brow" marks those properties: seeing the mountaintop as a brow marks its value for us, marks precisely those qualities of the unthinking that help us to think, marks the role it has in a dynamic interaction. The mountain plays a role in shaping the field we inhabit, just as a galaxy plays a role in shaping space-time.

It is worth pausing here to consider how the particular character of the Norwegian landscape has shaped the character of Norwegians' close involvement with nature. Christian Norberg-Schulz has outlined an answer to this question.

To . . . grasp the "anti-classical" spirit of the North, it is necessary to take a closer look at the Norwegian landscape. Although the country possesses a multitude of different regions, a kind of common denominator is everywhere present. We may suggest that it consists in a sort of "microstructure", that is, in an interminable variety of phenomena: the ground is rarely continuous, but is subdivided and has a varied relief; rocks and depressions, groves and glades, bushes and tufts of vegetation create a rich "world" of small elements. The sky is hardly experienced as a total hemisphere, but is narrowed down between the contours of trees and rocks, and is moreover continuously modified by clouds. The sun is relatively low and creates a rich play of patches of light and shadow, with clouds and vegetation acting as enriching "filters". Water is ever present as a dynamic element, both as running streams and quiet, reflecting ponds. The quality of the air is constantly changing, from moist fog to refreshing ozone. . . .

[28] "—More Mountains," from *Tenk på noe annet* [Think About Something Else] (1979); translation from *The Silence Afterwards: Selected Poems of Rolf Jacobsen*, trans. and ed. Roger Greenwald (Princeton: Princeton University Press, 1985), 249–51.

In general we may say that the Norwegian landscape is character-
ized by an infinite multitude of different places. Behind every hillock
and rock there is a new place, and only exceptionally is the landscape
unified to form a simple, univocal space. In this landscape, therefore,
man encounters a host of "forces", rather than the gods of the classical
world. . . .

We understand, therefore, that the Norwegian landscape demands
from man a different kind of adaptation from the landscape of the
classical South. . . . Nordic man has to approach nature through an act
of *empathy;* he has to live *with* nature in an intimate sense. Direct
participation is more important than the abstraction of an understood
order. This participation, however, is individual rather than social.
"My home is my castle" is in fact a Nordic saying. In Norway closeness
to nature means finding a place for oneself in the "wilderness", be-
tween rocks and dark, gloomy conifers, preferably next to a swift
stream of water. Thus the forces are mastered, and dwelling [is] real-
ized as an interaction between man and the given environment.[29]

This account makes it easy to see the connection between the physical
characteristics of Norwegian nature and the forms of some of Norway's
myths and folklore. What distinguishes Norway from most other modern
Western countries is that the evolution of thought there has gone on in
the heads of people who have continued to have direct knowledge of
nature and a close relation to it. But the Norwegian writer who incorpo-
rates that knowledge and experience in his work is apt to be viewed
either with condescension (by critics abroad, or by Norwegian critics
determined to be "sophisticated"), or with idealizing nostalgia (by Scan-
dinavians fond of the idea of innocent souls who arrive from field or hill
country "with their sacks full of nature, of unconscious, restorative gen-
ius, of cultural heritage and folk-myths and other wonderful things"[30]).

In Vesaas's poetry, an overwhelming majority of the nouns that name
concrete things name parts of nature. A count of such nouns in the poems
in this selection shows that seventy-five percent of them name parts of
nature; almost all the rest name objects of daily use, houses, or parts of
houses. I think these findings reveal a focus of interest rather than an
obliviousness to, or rustic escape from, the surfaces of modern life (how
readily one says "modern" when one means "urban").

[29] Christian Norberg-Schulz, "Living with Nature," *Swissair Gazette* 4/1985, 14.
[30] Hansen, "Fortælleren fra Vinje," 127.

Vesaas's traditional objects (and indeed, his natural phenomena) bear an already accreted meaning—at least to those who are still familiar with them. But he makes them carry a new world-picture. This achieves a double result. First, he finds an abyss at the center of the old phenomena, as so many moderns have done. At the same time, he finds a new kind of significance arising from the very interaction that uncovers the abyss:

> They're heavy as premonitions now,
> these houses that in daylight are friendly wood.
> > ("Late, in the Yard")

> Always that skewed house.
> With heavy thoughts read into it.
> > ("The Skewed House")

> Your still boat
> hasn't got a name.
> Your still boat
> hasn't got a port.
> Your secret boat on land.
> > ("The Boat on Land")

On the one hand, the abyss is all the more frightening for lying at the heart of the familiar, of what we have been used to trusting. On the other hand, the old vessels can carry more new meaning than newer vessels could have, and they establish a kind of continuity across the break that we think of as the modern. It is therefore worth asking whether the abyss that Vesaas confronts is the *same* one we usually meet in high modernism. Here are a few moments of what might seem to be dread manifesting through nature:

> What terrifies
> most of all,
> is the stone skulls in the beach.
> Mute grievers,
> a half-foot out of the ice,
> > ("Dead Lake")

> We felt a great pulse
> coming up from Death below.
> . . . .
> After that

there was the ocean.
The pulse and the ocean.

("The Boat")

The still eye under
the dark leaves.

("The Dark Eye")

One can feel here, I think, a strange calm that accompanies the fear. The abyss that opens here is not the void that lies beyond the limits of a solipsistic self. Rather, it is the depths of a whole that includes the self. So it is more terrifying for being within oneself, yet less terrifying because the self, through the sort of empathy that Norberg-Schulz refers to (and that Næss is much concerned with), is related to everything else. Rather than a void, the depths are a dark corner of a unified plenitude. Our fragmentary apprehension or understanding of that plenitude can cause terror, but one does not often meet despair here.

Nature functions on at least two levels in Vesaas's poetry. On the first, the poem evokes an experience in relation to nature that is revelatory of the relation and therefore of both nature and us. Almost any poem by Vesaas will illustrate this use of nature; and, as I have been arguing, many of the best Norwegian poets proceed from a grasp of such a relation. On the second level, Vesaas uses nature to get at another realm, at a range of meanings that lies beyond what we think of as the "actual." On this level, a vocabulary of responses connected to relations to nature enables Vesaas to convey meaning that lies even further beyond the reach of discursive paraphrase than the meaning in most poetry does. Such a vocabulary is analogous to the vocabulary of responses to music that an experienced listener acquires; and it poses problems for critics similar to those posed by music, which, being almost entirely nondenotative, is the quintessentially nondiscursive art form.

Just what the "other" realm or dimension is that Vesaas gets at, and where we are to locate it, are questions that have often vexed critics. Let us take one short poem by Vesaas, "Journey," and see where it leads us.

We finally appeared again
out of the night-fog.
And no one recognized anyone.
Underway we'd forgotten how.
Nor did anyone demand:

Who are you?

We couldn't have answered,
we had lost
our names.

Far off there was thunder
from an iron heart
that was always at work.
We listened without understanding.
We had come
farther than far.

Aside from the multiple contexts and their possible interrelationships that the poem suggests (a literal passage, probably by boat; a passage through a night of sleep or dream, or of sleepless vigil; through a time of war; through an experience of dissociation, or dissolving of the ego, or contact with some force beyond the rational), several features are worth remarking here. As we saw in "The Footprints," Vesaas's poems often render the moments just before something may (or may not) happen, or, as here, the moments just after something has happened. Hand in hand with this indirect temporal approach is the preponderance of negative assertions: no one recognized, no one asked, we couldn't have answered, we listened without understanding. This is typical of Vesaas's poetry; it would not surprise me if a concordance were to show that the most common word in the poems is the Norwegian for "not," followed closely by "no one," "nothing," and the adjectives that correspond to "silent, mute, secret, hidden, unknown, inexpressible, invisible."

The particular quality of Vesaas's negations is important to grasp. On the one hand, they are not of the mystical variety that *cancels* ordinary reality, regarding it as merely an illusion behind which a "true" transcendental reality is to be found. The journey, the fog, and the thunder retain their existence on the literal level. On the other hand, while Vesaas's negations have much in common *as method* with those of the best-known modern writers, the meanings they seem to get at—or, to be more circumspect, their attitudes toward meaning—are very different, as I have just suggested. For as Martin A. Hansen has pointed out, although Vesaas and other writers similarly situated share the "mark of proper writers in Europe" since the mid-nineteenth century—"perpetual wakefulness, sleepless thought, what one could call 'modern consciousness'"—they have not been "seduced by that metaphysical pessimism which has been so common elsewhere."[31]

The ending of "Journey" illustrates this point. The thunder is heard, the force behind it is sensed; that force turns out, in this instance, to suggest a heart, not a void. To listen without understanding is to do more than be enshrouded by the muffling fog; to know one does not understand is to have greater knowledge than one who is oblivious. That the final two lines echo a folktale formula suggests a connection to older accounts of discovery, a wry attitude toward any claim that the modern century has a patent on spiritual doubt or confrontations with the abyss. (These lines also remind us that Vesaas has roots in an oral tradition.) The language of the poem betrays no distrust of itself, no doubts that it can communicate, in its oblique way, to readers who will take it in—and can communicate, moreover, about something other than itself or the poet's consciousness.

As I remarked when I first considered Vesaas's modernity, his best poetry, like his best fiction, remains committed to a world much larger than himself to which he stands in dynamic interrelationship, and derives its power from the authenticity and acuity of his witness to that relationship. Writing about the fiction, Martin A. Hansen comments that the atmospheric power of Vesaas's portrayals "always achieves its highest degree in the pauses [characteristic] of his style. Through this silence he restores the sacral to the environment."[32] Kjølv Egeland has put a similar assessment in terms that are perhaps more readily applicable to the poetry: "Things are what they are, but also something other, something more. When everything clicks, the 'other' world merges with the 'real' one in a way that yields a revelation, at the same time as the whole is almost weirdly credible. Then we are truly 'beyond what can be said.'"[33]

The poems have, if anything, greater latitude than the fiction: they may retain only a minimal trace of the literal and still work; and when their symbols get out of hand, it is not by virtue of containing too little realistic reference, but by virtue of being vague or cliché, or too grand or too slight. Yet it seems to me that even when Vesaas uses abstractions, he is usually trying to get at an aspect of experienced reality, not at a mental construct. (It is precisely because we sense the implicit claim that he is

[31] Ibid., 126, 129.

[32] Ibid., 131.

[33] Kjølv Egeland, "Tarjei Vesaas," in *Norges litteraturhistorie* (Oslo: Cappelen, 1975), V: 176.

addressing real phenomena that we feel his writing is forced when it insists on meanings that strike us as "made up" or "read into" things.)

It is important to notice the quotation marks that Egeland uses around "real" and "other." Because we are *not* dealing with a mystical or transcendental dimension, there is no separation between "ordinary" phenomena and "other" phenomena that is intrinsic to the phenomena. There is a difference between our ability to perceive some types of significance and our ability to perceive other types—or at least between our ability to think discursively about the two types of perception. And there is greater ease in "testing" some types of perception than in testing others. But the difference is not one of kind. It is rather that our episteme, our language, and our culture encourage and train those abilities that perceive the so-called ordinary phenomena and discourage and ignore those abilities that perceive the so-called other—and this regime is what *makes* the "ordinary" ordinary and the "other" other. That is why the observation of "symbolic" elements in one of Vesaas's works can obscure the question of what sort of world that work as a whole conveys.

A symbol always has both abstract and concrete meanings. As Torben Brostrøm puts it, "The symbol is the unity of the symbolized and the symbolizing."[34] A particular symbol may seem more "abstract" than we feel metaphors generally are simply because we cannot easily "separate out" a concrete meaning—or because we rightly intuit that the symbol's use in context puts a heavier emphasis on its abstract part.[35] In either case, the use of the symbol in itself implies nothing about the attitude of the work toward "reality." To ask to what degree an author addresses the concrete world (in the sense conceived by realists) and to what degree the abstract, is to ask a different question from what the author's attitudes to both concrete and abstract are and how they function in his work. As long as we assume that *we* contribute to "outer" meanings, but insist on denying that the *environment* contributes to "inner" meanings, then, in dealing with Vesaas, we will have the feeling mentioned by Brostrøm, that we are tearing apart things that belong together—precisely the feeling Næss also alludes to after citing the lines of verse about the birch tree.

Resistance to the idea that nature is animate (inspirited), or has an

[34] Brostrøm, "Tarjei Vesaas's symbolverden belyst ud fra hans prosaværker 1940–50," *Edda* (1955), 35.

[35] See Owen Barfield, *Speaker's Meaning* (Middletown, CT: Wesleyan University Press, 1967, rpt. 1984), 59–61.

"inside," runs deep in our culture (as my earlier reference to "accusations" of animism implied). Ironically, this resistance is particularly strong among Norwegian critics of the past thirty years. Their commitment to materialist philosophies (or ideologies) and their determination to lay the ghost of National Romanticism have made the discussion of spirit, especially in connection with nature, taboo. For example, Tor Ulven, in his engaging article on Vesaas's poetry, outlines clearly what I regard as a false dichotomy.

> Landscape as a stage for poetic transformations and revelations has a long tradition in poetry, and landscape is also the most frequent starting point for themes in Vesaas. The visionary landscape tradition is especially strong in Nynorsk lyric poetry, and in poets such as Olav Aukrust (1883–1929) and Olav Nygard (1884–1924) the metaphysical revelations of nature appear as the climactic point of poetry. The same cannot be said of Vesaas. He retains the mystery, but moves it from a divine sphere to the human mind. If he describes a collapsed face in a mountain, or says that "the lake is breathing tonight," it is not because the poet believes that some supernatural power is using nature in order to give signs. That is why Vesaas's landscape metaphors are so convincing: it is we who see nature open up, and it closes into meaninglessness again behind us as soon as we have moved on.[36]

One could as well say that life represents nature moving through us, and that when it has moved on, we become meaningless. (Certainly nature retains its *coherence* after we move on.) But it is more fruitful to say that people and nature move through each other, and indeed, shape the "field" in which both move. It is noteworthy that the only alternative Ulven sees to the interpretation of nature as divine emblem is one that posits humans alone as the source of any meaning to be found in symbols made from nature. That he in fact wishes to exclude not only God, but any spiritual dimension, becomes clear in a later passage:

> [M]uch of Vesaas's poetry seems mysterious and tempts one to close reading. The problem (and the strength) in a good poem is that it survives by virtue of its ultimately indissoluble images. . . . [A] good poem's images (visual or not) can never be translated into purely conceptual language. This phenomenon becomes clear in many of

[36] Ulven, "Hjem til det ukjente," 79–80.

Vesaas's poems. Close reading can never get close enough, but this has nothing to do with any putative spirituality.[37]

Earlier critics seem to have felt less constrained, as my quotations from Martin A. Hansen show. The Norwegian novelist Johan Borgen, writing about Vesaas's fiction, went into some detail about "mystery."

[W]hat I would like to get said is that Vesaas uses purely rational means to conjure up his mystery.

Perhaps someone will protest against the word mystery, in the belief that mystery must be mystical. But utterly clear mystery is a part of Tarjei Vesaas's material. The forests in Vesaas are pregnant with mystery. People's steps in the forest have a life of their own. If a person afraid of the dark begins to tread cautiously among the trees, then all the evil forces are set loose; someone is walking alongside him. But in better times no one is walking alongside the road in Vesaas; no one is threatening, there are just trees alongside the road . . . , woodwinds. What I am trying to convey is that the phenomena really *live* in Vesaas's forest—fear or fanfares. His climate is peopled, or shall we say inspirited, never illustrated. His landscape is pregnant with action beforehand. Only a touch is needed! A twig breaks, and the drama is under way! And what does "beforehand" mean? That the writer *knows* the landscape, the spirits. The writer's mind *exists* there; this writer is no nature fancier, no tourist or observer.[38]

Brikt Jensen, writing about the same novel, *Is-slottet* (*The Ice Palace*), insists that the book is not a psychological study in the traditional sense.

[37] Ibid., 83. Later in the same essay, in a discussion of the poem "Vi fyller dei vidaste nettene" ("We Fill the Widest Nights"), Ulven remarks that the glass mountain represents wholeness (among other things), as against humans' conflict-laden splits. He comments: "In Vesaas's work humans have definitively stepped out of the totality of nature (except possibly on the level of momentary experience), and it is perhaps precisely this separateness and the quality of being split that make humans what they are. Those who would like, nostalgically, to reintegrate humanity in a natural (and cosmic) harmony of wholeness will hardly find encouragement in this poem. Here as elsewhere, the author consistently insists on the tensions, without any wish to dissolve them in some macrosymphony of the spheres" (86). I find Ulven's reading of the poem perceptive, but cannot accept the conflation of wholeness and harmony, the assumption that no notion of wholeness can be modern, or in general the either-or framework that Ulven uses.
[38] Johan Borgen, "Slottet Vesaas bygget," in *Tarjei Vesaas*, ed. Jan Erik Vold (Oslo: Kulturutvalget i Det Norske Studentersamfund, 1964), 168.

Instead of proceeding analytically, building a view of a person by accumulating small observations and explaining them, Vesaas

> unfolds a soul for us and lets its many idiosyncrasies take shape in images. Or rather, he builds on an abundance of visual images from the Norwegian winter landscape, but puts the details together in such a way that they give as strong an impression of soul as of nature. People learn to know themselves through the impressions of nature they dwell upon.[39]

The word "soul" sounds archaic and even suspect to us now in English, but it is still used in other Germanic languages to refer to the totality of inner being, and it does not necessarily have religious connotations. I do not think that the earlier critics I have cited accounted for Vesaas's achievements in the way they did because they adhered to certain belief systems. Rather, I think they gave accounts that conveyed the feeling of how Vesaas affected them as readers, and they used terms that seemed appropriate to the means Vesaas used and the vision those means derived from. These critical accounts seem notably unconstrained by dogma.

For purposes of placing Vesaas on a poetic map broader than the Norwegian one, it will help to find some coordinates in better-known territory. A comparison of Vesaas and two American poets with whom he shares certain traits will help delineate those traits, at the same time as it will reveal important differences that set Vesaas apart. Vesaas has much in common with William Carlos Williams, in particular Williams's recognition of a spirit in the world[40] and a sensitivity to that spirit, which M. L. Rosenthal called "empathic responsiveness."[41] To a considerable extent, the approach or stance of the two poets has similar consequences for the role of the speaker in the poems. Stang remarks that Vesaas's lyric poetry

> is not a "personal lyric" akin to Romantic Expressionist poetry. Vesaas's pronoun is not *I*, but one—you—we. One could call his poetry pragmatic; one senses a strong ethical appeal: you shall, you must realize.[42]

[39] Brikt Jensen, "Is-slottet," *Syn og segn* (1963), 447.

[40] I have already quoted part of Breslin's description of this; see Breslin, *William Carlos Williams*, x–xi.

[41] Rosenthal, *The Modern Poets*, 115.

[42] Stang, "Lyrikken," 247.

Breslin writes of Williams:

> Internally, Williams puts himself at the edge of consciousness, where "light becomes / darkness and darkness / light"—where experience becomes at once fluid and distinct; Williams's mockery of the "I" is not a repudiation of individuality but of that hard assertiveness which negates all sympathetic receptivity.[43]

> Williams's work has the impersonality and objectivity of a great deal of modern art; but it is special in that self-effacement works for him as part of a process of maintaining intimacy with immediate experience and thus of evolving true individuality.[44]

These descriptions could as well be applied to Vesaas. But where Breslin finds in Williams a "[d]escent into the body [that] takes us back to the primordial unity where distinctions between inner and outer, self and object, do not yet exist,"[45] I find in Vesaas a "descent" into the world and a continual apprehension of the tension between interrelating inner and outer, self and object. Vesaas's work, like Williams's, "tries to draw us down into this intense consciousness."[46] Yet in Vesaas we sense that imagination takes us not so much into "the deeper consciousness hidden in the body"[47] as into the deeper consciousness hidden in the world, or rather in the relation between self and world.

The two approaches are quite close, as one can see in Breslin's account of the difference between Williams on the one hand and Pound and Eliot on the other.

> [T]he difference between adopting tradition or place as the creative source is that the ground is available to anyone who will look under his bootsoles. Williams speaks from a crude locus—in the earth and in the body—that is potentially, if not actually, common. It is by adopting this physical perspective that Williams deals with the modern breakdown of belief; he can now claim to be articulating a kind of consciousness that is buried in all of us.[48]

---

[43] Breslin, *William Carlos Williams*, 75.
[44] Ibid., 35.
[45] Ibid., 44.
[46] Ibid.
[47] Ibid., 47.
[48] Ibid., 47–48.

Vesaas's advantage vis-à-vis his readers—that his locus in the earth actually *was* common property—is a disadvantage vis-à-vis his critics, who, as I have pointed out, associate responsiveness to nature with the (often sentimental) idealizing of National Romanticism. Vesaas draws on the same contact with nature that most earlier Norwegian poetry played on, but he puts that contact to a radically new use.

His articulation of a "deeper consciousness" that often seems mysterious gives Vesaas one central achievement in common with a more recent American poet who is in other respects almost his opposite: John Ashbery. I choose to make the contrast because I think it illustrates in particular the way in which Vesaas draws on experiences in nature.

Ashbery seems to render a deep meditative, reflective, or sometimes ruminative process without "translating" that process into higher-level cognitive terms. Vesaas too conveys the rhythms and apprehensions of something deep in people and the world without "translating" that depth into cognitive or abstract terms; the "something" is not meditation, but a state of being. That is, where Ashbery's depth is psychological, Vesaas's is spiritual (in the sense defined earlier).[49] Moreover, where Ashbery's meditations appear mainly as a process that involves some "place" deep inside people, Vesaas's states of being inevitably involve a relation between a "place" deep inside people and a much larger world they find themselves in.

Both Vesaas and Ashbery render "untranslatable" levels of inner life, but they use almost opposite means. Ashbery uses the syntax and some of the vocabulary of discourse to convey inner movements of mind and feeling that not only are nondiscursive, but seem almost subverbal; the importance of visual art to his work is well known. Vesaas uses the syntax and vocabulary of oral narrative and injected commentary to render movements of spirit or being that are similarly subverbal; his imagery leans toward the aural rather than the visual. The ways in which these poets use nature are also opposite. In Ashbery, the elements of the natural world that turn up in the poems are openly fictive, contrived for the purpose of concretizing meaning that derives from the interior events with which nature is compared. In Vesaas, on the other hand, one always feels that nature imagery, however simplified or transformed it may be, draws on real nature, and that it brings a meaning of its own to the task

[49] Once one grasps the difference between Vesaas and the mainstream of modernism, one realizes that a term like "existential" would be too narrow here and would carry the wrong philosophical baggage.

of conveying the qualities of interior events. Vesaas could count on his readers' familiarity with the tonal palette of real nature and its connections to a spectrum of feeling. Ashbery is reflexive, Vesaas allusive. (Vesaas, as well as other Norwegian poets, thus has allusion in common with Chinese and Japanese poetry, with the difference that in these the allusions are often conventionalized and refer as much to a long poetic tradition as to experiences in nature shared by the reader.)

Here, to give just one example, is a short passage from Ashbery's long poem "Clepsydra," followed by the opening and closing of Vesaas's "Shadows on the Point":

> It was the long way back out of sadness
> Of that first meeting: a half-triumph, an imaginary feeling
> Which still protected its events and pauses, the way
> A telescope protects its view of distant mountains
> And all they include, the coming and going,
> Moving correctly up to other levels, preparing to spend the night
> There where the tiny figures halt as darkness comes on,
> Beside some loud torrent in an empty yet personal
> Landscape, which has the further advantage of being
> What surrounds without insisting, the very breath so
> Honorably offered, and accepted in the same spirit.
> There was in fact pleasure in those high walls.
> Each moment seemed to bore back into the centuries
> For profit and manners, and an old way of looking that
> Continually shaped those lips into a smile. Or it was
> Like standing at the edge of a harbor early on a summer morning
> With the discreet shadows cast by the water all around
> And a feeling, again, of emptiness, but of richness in the way
> The whole thing is organized, on what a miraculous scale,
> Really what is meant by a human level, with the figures of giants
> Not too much bigger than the men who have come to petition
>   them. . . .[50]

[From "Shadows on the Point"]
Black shadows slide around the point with no let-up
and without a sound,
    for that's what it's like in our minds.

[50] Ashbery, *Rivers and Mountains* (New York: Holt, Rinehart and Winston, 1966), 29–30.

That's how we've gathered at the point
as the day ebbs.
And as the light ebbs
we stand all the more still,
without saying why.
Stiller and stiller
on our point.

. . .

But at any rate we can't stay here
on the point—
We're just standing here waiting for something new.
Rivers go drifting past every scorched point,
and on the point the shadows stand ashamed
and wait for the boat.
The oarless boat is our fate.
All steering taken from us.

We stand here in your deep night, Night,
and wait for something new from beyond the point.
The current runs black and silent.
And what we feel through it
we don't tell each other.

Ashbery's poems (like those of Stevens before him) often point up the
hypothetical status of their images (e.g. *"some* loud torrent"): "or it was
like standing" not only carries the inherent distance of simile, but reminds
us that there is a poet at work who is choosing to make comparisons.
Vesaas's poems rarely carry such explicit self-references, though occa-
sional comments in a suddenly colloquial tone may remind us of the
poet's presence.[51] Nor does Vesaas suggest that he could as well have
chosen a different image: part of his art is to uncover *necessary* connec-
tions, and (as I remarked earlier) if a poem of his fails to convince us
about necessity, we are apt to find it forced. Yet this difference does not
mean Vesaas's poems are unaware of how they work or fail to give the

[51] See Stang, "Lyrikken," 237. The reader may find it of interest to compare Vesaas's
poem "The Mountain That Wept" to Stevens's "The Poem That Took the Place of a
Mountain"; and Vesaas's "The Boat on Land" to a remarkably similar untitled late poem
by Neruda that begins, "This broken bell" (see Pablo Neruda, *The Sea and the Bells*, trans.
William O'Daly [Port Townsend: Copper Canyon, 1988], 67).

reader any help in seeing how they work. It is to be expected that, as the method is so different, the pointers to it will also be different.

Vesaas is not alone among Norwegian poets in guiding the reader to the *premises* on which his poetry rests, rather than to the details of the process by which it is created. Rolf Jacobsen, for example, concludes a poem called "Day and Night" this way:

> There is no end to the stars and the wind.
> There is only you yourself
> who aren't who you think you are.[52]

One way of glossing this is: "You are mistaken if you think natural phenomena end; you are what ends. And you are mistaken if you think you are *just* you, rather than part of a relation to those phenomena."

When one has read Vesaas's poetry and grasped intuitively his special mode of apprehension and expression, one returns to the first poem in his first book of poems to find, perhaps with some surprise, that what may at first have appeared to be Romantic or sentimental is in fact an emotionally charged but nonetheless clear statement of the premises underlying his world view and his work. "Snow and spruce forest" is a gestalt that is both outside and inside "us." It is both starting point and end point. It is "home" because "it has its place in us" even before we are told what it is—i.e., before it has a *name* that we can grasp intellectually. That the landscape lives inside us and we live in the landscape is the fundamental intimacy of contact that is Vesaas's starting point as well as the basis of his symbolic language. Stang remarks:

> What the poet does is to remove layer upon layer of abstraction and thereby reestablish the connection between the name and the thing's being. Our language has developed in the direction of greater and greater abstraction. When we say "snow," it is a concept for us; it includes all forms of snow. But the *experience* of snow as it was for us when we saw [snow] is lost in the process.[53]

Quoting the Danish poet Paul la Cour, Stang suggests that what Vesaas manages to do here is to reestablish the lost intensity between words and things, and that he does this through his use of the image. Yet as Stang herself admits, this description could be applied to much modern poetry, and indeed, to much earlier poetry.

[52] Jacobsen, *The Silence Afterwards*, 59.
[53] Stang, "Lyrikken," 229.

"Snow and Spruce Forest" is in fact a poem in which the imagery is fairly conventional, even down to the topos of fire and ice near the end. What the poem achieves, it achieves through statement, through the "logic" of its development, through a spiraling structure that makes good use of repetition, through cleanly honed language, through rhythms that embody both the thought and the feelings in the poem, and through allusion to a world of experience that the reader must either have to begin with or must gain knowledge of from the work itself. Once we have such knowledge, this poem rings clear. But if we are not equipped to grasp what underlies the poem, we will see it as conventional or sentimental.

It is worth noting that although "Snow and Spruce Forest" refers to a kind of experience and a kind of knowledge that we have as children, it moves to a conscious adult grasp of these things. Indeed, the poem suggests that it is only by virtue of travel and return that we can grasp the meaning of "home," that only adult experience can bestow significance on our starting points and yield understanding of that significance. This theme is taken up again in "Through Naked Branches," a remarkable contemplation on fulfillment in the face of oncoming death. Watching the bare branches of a tree fade in the twilight outside his window, the speaker says:

> You think it's as if you
> have always seen your life through
> supple, naked branches,
> and coarse branches with thick bark.
> An entanglement of air and life
> and everything that flows.

The entanglement (or more literally, "inter-filtering") is indeed such that it cannot be teased apart, for "entanglement" here refers to the network of branches (which contains a flowing life of its own), to the life of the speaker (which flows among the branches just as the air does), and to the whole way in which "you / have always seen your life"; while the word "life" in "air and life" includes the entanglement. So these apparently simple lines become complexly recursive and thus embody the sort of interrelationship they refer to.

The speaker proceeds to a moving image.

> The still network of branches grows dimmer
> each time I look up.

It's resting in friendly dusk.
I think it is blooming inside me
because I have always loved it.

This calm apprehension of a natural cycle that implicitly includes death, and the striking empathic inclusiveness that makes the growth of new life in the trees in March (as the season's light increases) a kind of blossoming in the speaker (as the light of day and of life diminishes), are nothing like a "dreamlike uniting of self and object."[54] For knowledge of interrelationship is not a dream; as Næss points out, the self and the object are not separate in quite the way the ostensible "uniting" assumes.[55] It is misleading and ultimately fruitless to assign the term "transcendental" to Vesaas's way of *understanding* life, both because the term carries connotations (whether of fantasy or faith) that derive from the dominant opposite view (just as "pathetic" carries the connotations given it by rationalists), and because the entire axis defined by the poles immanence/transcendence is merely a line within the field of relations in which Vesaas moves.[56]

If Vesaas's poems do not unite subject and object in a dreamlike mode, nor do they do so in a dissociative mode—that is, by dissolving an alien-

[54] See Walter Baumgartner, "Slik var den draumen: Om Tarjei Vesaas som visjonær," trans. Leif Mæhle, in *Norsk litterær årbok 1970* (Oslo: Det Norske Samlaget, 1970), 24–25; and the commentary on this article in Henning K. Sehmsdorff, "Tagore og Vesaas: Påvirkning eller slektskap?" in *Norsk litterær årbok 1982* (Oslo: Det Norske Samlaget, 1982), 41–42. I have quoted Sehmsdorff's (accurate) characterization of Baumgartner's view. The poem I have quoted here contains a hidden "middle" element of empathic identification, that of the speaker with his house. For it is a common spring custom in Norway, as in many other countries, to bring budding branches indoors and put them in water so they may bloom there.

[55] Næss offers the fascinating example of a Sami who stood accused in a Norwegian court of demonstrating illegally at a river (a planned hydroelectric project there threatened the habitat of reindeer). The Sami "said that the part of the river in question was 'part of himself.'" Næss explores why various reformulations of this statement aimed at making it "intellectually more understandable" are inadequate. "We intuitively grasp," Næss says, "roughly what [the Sami] means. But it is of course difficult to elucidate the meaning in philosophical or psychological terminology" (*Self-realization*, 7, 9 [unpag.]).

[56] To use an analogy, it would be equally misleading to assign the term "magical" or "supernatural" to a yogi's ability to control his heartbeat or his brain waves. At a certain time, the conceptual framework of Western medicine saw such control as a violation of the distinction between autonomic and voluntary functions. But for the yogi, such control is a (fairly trivial) consequence of *knowledge* of the *relation* between mind and body.

ated subject in the surroundings. Almost every poem in the present selection has either a narrative or a discursive structure. (By the latter I mean a structure built up of statements that follow one upon the other; I do not mean the statements should be taken discursively.) There may be small leaps in both time and logic, or the paths followed by action or thought may not be straight lines, but the frameworks are there and usually quite clear. This means that structurally the poems work in a way that is virtually the opposite of the predominant modern style, the development of which Donoghue (following leads from McLuhan) traces from landscape through landscape painting to interior or psychological landscape. Donoghue points out that both Tennyson and Eliot

> establish a landscape which corresponds so intimately to a 'state of mind' that it becomes that state, for the life of the poem. It is worth remarking that both poets had the same temperamental difficulty in going beyond these states of mind to render states of being; what we call 'the world's body', the sense of being and character, of which a state of mind is only one part, one moment.[57]

It is Louis Simpson's view that "[t]here has been very little poetry in English that represents states of being. Wordsworth's is the only great poetry in English to have done so."[58]

This comment underscores how it is possible for Vesaas to start with landscape and end up with poems that probe spirit or being. A typical short poem by Vesaas is, at its deepest, neither narrative nor lyric, no matter what its surface structure may be, but rather a sort of "core" of a moment, like the core of soil or stone or ice that geologists extract. The poem yields, in layers, temporal, natural, psychological, social, and mythical contexts. Taken together, these render the states of being—or in my sense, the spiritual contexts—that contribute powerfully to the uniqueness of Vesaas's poems. Two poets' eyes may see much the same thing, but silent excavation of the moment's spirit proceeds from somewhere invisible, somewhere uncharted except in the distinct ways the poet has drawn for himself. Vesaas's well-known poem, "Rain in Hiroshima," for example, is important not for its political content, which is common-

---

[57] Donoghue, *Ordinary Universe*, 97.

[58] Louis Simpson, "Poetry Chronicle," *Hudson Review* 16, No. 1 (spring 1963), rpt. as "Silence in the Snowy Fields," in Simpson, *A Company of Poets* (Ann Arbor: University of Michigan Press, 1981), 79.

place, but because it manages to take a "core" of the immeasurable, the unfathomable.

In one remarkable poem, which we can now attempt to understand, Vesaas goes so far as to probe our relation to nature from nature's node in the field. In the poem "A Little Disturbance," a child gets lost in a broad meadow; the poet compares this to an ocean and wonders if the child imagines it is "moving in that strange world / it was in before it was born." Blond hair appears now and then "amid wild chervil / and vetch," then disappears. The poem says the child "will die in its flower-bed / in quiet wonder." "No one will find it until mowing time."

What is the point of view in this poem? One critic remarks that we do not experience the situation from the inside, but through a consciousness that registers what happens.[59] But whose consciousness can that be? Any person witnessing that hair appearing and vanishing would act to save the child. Of course this approach is literal-minded; why shouldn't a poet, contemplating the discovery of a lost child's body, imagine how the tragedy came about. This may well be how the poem came into being; on the other hand, it could just as well have originated as a parable about the limited understanding and short life-span of human beings lost in the natural world. But the important issue is not how the poem started, but what it became. Vesaas writes it in the perfect, present, and future tenses; it is more prospective than retrospective. And it does not, indeed cannot, represent the view of a human observer. Yet its physical details are so vivid that the poem in no way presents itself as supposition, as an imagined scenario. We are shown what happens and told what will happen, but no eyes see this. The poem does not have a point of *view*; it has an angle of knowledge. Only nature itself can "know" what the child does among the roots of plants. In this unusual poem *the setting* gets outside itself and "looks" at itself. (This makes sense of the title: it is the setting that is disturbed slightly.) It is because nature has an inside (as Barfield puts it) that the inside can become an outside here.

Such an analysis takes us to the edges of Vesaas's strangeness—yet only to reveal aspects fundamental to much of his best work. If one looks hard at Vesaas's poetry, one realizes that it is difficult to place on our maps of modern literature not because it is not modern, but because the maps need to be redrawn. Or, to switch to an appropriately aural metaphor,

[59] Steinar Gimnes, "Nærleik og avstand: Eg-et og omverda i Tarjei Vesaas' lyrikk," in *Norsk litterær årbok 1973* (Oslo: Det Norske Samlaget, 1973), 28.

the key signature of poets like Vesaas lies in a range we are perfectly capable of hearing, but have grown unaccustomed to. This fact, combined with the natural tendency of critical discussions of depth to focus on "content" that can be stated discursively, leaves many who try to account for the depth of Vesaas's work struggling for words. Yet as new models for thinking about our relation to our world make headway, critics will no doubt find ways of dealing with poetry like Vesaas's that are consistent with our apprehension of the poems. We will then be better equipped to evaluate the achievement of many Scandinavian poets in an international context.

Roger Greenwald

THROUGH NAKED BRANCHES

FRÅ

Kjeldene
1946

FROM

The Sources
1946

Snø og granskog

Tale om heimsleg—
snø og granskog
er heimsleg.

Frå første stund
er det vårt.
Før nokon har fortalt det,
at det *er* snø og granskog,
har det plass i oss—
og sidan er det der
heile heile tida.

Meterdjup fonn
kring mørke tre
—det er for oss!
Innblanda i vår eigen ande.
Heile heile tida,
om ingen ser det,
har vi snø og granskog med.

Ja lia med snøen,
og tre ved tre
så langt ein ser,
kvar vi er
vender vi mot det.

Og har i oss ein lovnad
om å koma heim.
Koma heim,
gå borti der,
bøyge greiner,
—og kjenne så det fer i ein
kva det er å vera der ein høyrer til.

Snow and Spruce Forest

Talk about what home is—
snow and spruce forest
is home.

From the very start
it is ours.
Before anyone has told us
that it *is* snow and spruce forest,
it has its place in us—
and then it is there
the whole, whole time.

Waist-high drift
around dark trees
—it's here for ús!
Mixed into our own breath.
The whole, whole time,
though no one sees it,
we have snow and spruce forest with us.

Yes, the hill under snow,
and tree upon tree
as far as you gaze—
wherever we are
we find ourselves
facing this.

And have in us a promise
about coming home.
Coming home,
going out there,
bending branches,
—and feeling so it flares in you
what it is to be where you belong.

Heile heile tida,
til det er sløkt
i våre innlandshjarte.

The whole, whole time,
until it's put out
in our inland hearts.

Snø i eit andlet

Det drys nok ned som ei himmelsk ville,
men mørkret gøymer bort alt i kveld.
Og ingen larm blandar opp det stille
usynlege singlet av snø som fell.

Her stegar på vegen så ingen veit det.
Går ein gut, og så ingen fleir.
Han går frå fest, langs det kvite leite.
Går bort frå eit auge som ville *meir.*

Bort frå den fagre draumen bak linet
som aldri har hetna i honoms hand.
Men auga i kveld var så rart i skinet.
Det kom med bod ifrå lova land.

Stille drevet silar langs kjaken,
rispar han lint med sitt stjerneris.
Gleda går gjennom natta naken.
Andletet brenn under bråna is.

Snow in a Face

It's sifting down like a jumbled heaven,
but the darkness tonight hides everything from view.
And there's no noise to break up the even
invisible tinkling of falling snow.

Walking the road so no one knows it,
one boy goes by, and that's all.
He's coming from a party, along the white hillside,
away from a glance that wanted *more*.

Away from the beautiful dream beneath the linen,
a dream that's never flamed in his hands.
But the glance tonight had a strange gleam in it;
came with a message from a promised land.

The quiet flakes float along his jawline,
gently scratch him with their switch of stars.
Delight is walking naked in the nighttime.
His face is burning as the snow dissolves.

Mars 1945

Enn er der ljos i roma,
om det er blivi meir enn kveld.
No gjeld det å arbeide
før alt bryt ut i eld.

Visst er det *det* som nagar
og skaper dette døyve jag:
Det kan ikkje bli ferdig—
I dag er siste dag.

I natt vil ordet koma
som gneiste over tusen mil:
Gå ut til kamp, så sant som du
vil høyre landet til!

Det pustar bortimellom,
av liv som søv i marsgrå natt.
Søv og hentar styrke.
Kor mange vil bli att?

No søv dei som ein nåde.
I skogen andre søv på bar.
No ropar mælet utan stans
om det å vera klar.

March 1945

Though it's way past bedtime
there's still light in the rooms.
Now there's work to do
before all hell breaks loose.

Of course that's what nags at you
and makes this smothered rush:
Today's the last day—
It can't be done.

Tonight the word will come,
flashed across a thousand miles:
Go out to battle, if you really
want to be part of this country!

The breathing's everywhere
of lives that sleep this gray March night.
Sleep and gather strength.
How many will be spared?

Now their sleep is mercy.
In the forest others sleep on needles.
Now the voice is calling constantly
to be ready.

Mørke skip innover

I lummer midnatt sig det liksom skip
innover himmelsletta langt der sør.
Dei dukkar opp, med sine helvet gøymt
bak blygrå sider. Allting søv som før.

Tungt ladde skuggar utan stans i leia,
men alfort stille om si løynde last.
Snart er dei ordna over dimme nattland.
—I vonde draumar blir du halden fast.

For eingong kom det slik på *havsens* flod.
Ei vårnatt. Til eit land som sov i fred.
Du ser det og du ser det gjennom draumen—
og kjenner atter angest gå i skred.

Alt vev seg saman i ditt heite kammer,
så lufta blir for kvæv å puste i.
Det kjem når tunge sider sig på himlen.
Aldri blir du kvitt det i di tid.

Dark Ships Coming

On a sultry midnight the clouds spread like ships
over the plain of the sky, far south.
They loom up, with their fury concealed
behind gun-gray sides. And life's asleep.

Heavily laden shadows coursing without pause
but keeping still about their secret freight.
Soon they're arrayed over the dim night country.
—Terrible dreams grip you tight.

Because once they came like this on the *ocean's* tide.
On a spring night. To a land that slept in peace.
You see it and you see it through the dream—
and again you feel the terror crack and slide.

Everything tangles together in your hot room,
so the air gets too close to breathe in.
It comes when ironclads spread over the sky.
You'll never shake it as long as you live.

Hesten

Dagen var heit og lang—no skal han gå.
No er det kveld, og alle ljod er få.
Ei smågjente labbar inn døra naken: Godnatt til far!
Ho smeller ein kyss, og går til sitt svale putevar.

Han går ikkje sjølv. Stilnar til. Ved eit rotet bord.
Papir og bøker. Skrevne og prenta ord.
Gjentekyssen på kinnet var varm og rund,
men gløymest likevel bort i same stund.

No er det arbeid. Og tida får gå som ho vil.
Omsider han ser mot ruta—og rykker til:
Ute er mørkt. Då kan ein arbeide best.
—Men no ligg det inn på ruta eit andlet: Ein hest!

Eit veldig hestandlet. Grått som leir.
Med svarte djupe auge. Ein ser ikkje meir.
Og ikkje ei rørsle i det. Men heile ruta dekt.
—Ein faren, underleg tidbolk blir oppatt vekt.

Han stirer på synet. Ja! hesten *er* grå.
Mange slitsame dagar såg denna attende på
då han vart skoten bak gjerdet. Med krøkte kne
låg han velt der i kleggsurr. Far stod gripen attved.

Kring denna gråe hesten var allting arbeid og onn.
Vognrammel, solsteik, høylukt, regn, vassing i fonn.
Taumen fila den unge handa. Ho lære fekk
i alle årstider det å styre ein hest som gjekk og gjekk.

—Og no er han komen på ruta. Og kallar fram
alt som var rikt og enkelt, i trollande ham.
Å nei, det er ikkje for moro. Ikkje kjem han med fred.
Spursmålet står inn strengt og stumt: Kva driv du med?

The Horse

The day was hot and long—now it's going.
Evening: the sounds are small and far between.
A little girl pads into the room naked: Goodnight to father!
She smacks a kiss, and goes off to her cool pillow.

He stays. Quiets down. At a messy table.
Paper and books. Written and printed words.
The girl's kiss on his cheek was warm and round,
but nonetheless forgotten in a moment.

Now it's work. And time can run by as it pleases.
At length he looks toward the window—and startles:
It's dark out. That's the best time for work.
—But now there's a face against the window: A horse!

A huge horse's face. Gray as clay.
With black deep eyes. That's all you see.
And not the slightest movement. But the whole pane filled.
—A shadowy, vanished time returns, unreels.

He stares at the vision. Yes! the horse *is* gray.
This one had many weary days to look back on
when he was shot behind the fence. With bent knees
he lay overturned, in a drone of horseflies. Father stood by, moved.

Around this gray horse everything was sweat and toil.
Wagon-clatter, broiling sun, smell of hay, rain, slogging through snow.
The rein rasped a young hand. Which learned the trick
to guiding, in all seasons, a horse that trudged and trudged.

—And now he's come to the window. And calls up,
enchanted, all that was rich and simple.
Ah no, it's not for fun. He hasn't come in peace.
The mute question bears down: What is it you do?

Kva gjer du ved detta bordet? Er du klar
til møte som barn som før, med alt du har?
Det skjer gjennom ord og papir. Det trenger inn
til det som det gjeld om bakom: heilt sinn.

Kva kan han svara? Det er som allting lyer.
Han ser mot det mørke auga, og angest sigler som skyer.
Det er hans eiga store og dyre barneverd
som no har møtt opp med hesten og går han nær.

Då møter frå verda *no* det reinaste: Far, godnatt!
Og trykket av lepper på kinnet synest å vera der att.
Velsigna den som strålar ut kraft frå si pute.
Hesten får stå der han står med spursmål ute.

What are you doing at this table? Are you ready
to meet, as the child you were, with everything you are?
It cuts through words and paper. It seeps down
to what it's about underneath: the core of him.

What can he answer? Everything's waiting to hear.
He looks toward the dark eyes, and fear comes sailing like clouds:
His own wide and precious childhood world
appeared with the horse, and now it closes in.

Then meets the simplest part of *this* world: Father, goodnight!
And the pressure of lips on his cheek seems beyond doubt.
Bless the girl who radiates strength from her pillow.
The horse can stay where he is with his question: shut out.

FRÅ

Leiken og lynet
1947

FROM

The Game and the Lightning
1947

Lomen går mot nord

Høgt som prikkar mot skyene,
einsame endå dei er tvo,
går lomane nordover
og blir borte.

Berre eit kjøleg skrik
når ned frå dei
dit vi står fast
i vårt store virrvarr.

Men ute av syne
styrer dei loddrett ned
i ein iskald sjø
som har vekt hemmeleg varme.

Slikt høyrer vi gjerne—
eit einsamt vilt hjarta
som i grenselaus fridom
endå søker ned til oss.

The Loons Head North

So high they're dots against the clouds,
lonely even if they're two,
the loons head north
and are gone.

Only one cool cry
reaches down from them
to where we're stuck
in our great muddle.

But out of sight
they steer straight down
into an ice-cold lake
that's aroused hidden warmth.

This we'll gladly hear—
a lonely, wild heart
that in limitless freedom
still finds its way to us.

Vårlukten

Er alt fortrolla
av vårens ange?
No må hjarte le,
og auge sjå for sant:

Dessa seljetrea frå ein var liten,—
no står dei med veldige kroner,
svimrande ange-kroner
den eine utanpå den andre,
—lauvkrona som kvart jordisk auga ser
er berre ei kjerne.

Blågrått him
over øre marker.
Bylgjer over drukne hus.
Og svartjorda gøymd i solrøyk
gjennomhola av fuglesong
til glitrande sold kvar morgon.

Brune kyr på bakken
i sig hit og dit,
med uskulds fagre ro,
med håse raut
inni store oppstigande kuplar
av varm dyre-eim.

Og unge menneske
inni lette klotar av innbilling,
søtare enn selje-kroner,
i vandring til underlege møte.
Og angen
av hold og hår og lin og draum
komande og gåande
i stunder
når ingen får sova.

The Smell of Spring

Is everything bewitched
by the smell of spring?
The heart has to laugh now
and the eyes admit:

These willow trees from when you were little—
now they've got giant crowns,
dizzying crowns of fragrance
enveloping each other,
—the leafy top that shows itself
to our sight
is only the core.

Blue-gray mist
over giddy fields.
Billows over drunken houses.
And black earth hidden
in a heat-haze riddled by birdsong:
a glittering mesh every morning.

Brown cows on the hill
drifting to and fro
with the lovely calm of innocence,
with hoarse mooing
inside huge ascending domes
of warm animal-steam.

And young people
within mild globes of imagining
sweeter than willow-crowns,
rambling toward mysterious meetings.
And the scent
of flesh and hair and linen and dream
coming and going
at times
when no one can sleep.

Eit ord om hausten

Så var det komi
til september.
Vart glødande september.
Stilt og klårt mellom fjella,
og klårt over.

Svære rom av klårt
var ute farande,
og inni der
ringde septemberklokka
til arbeids møde.

Vi gjekk til jorda.
Til alles jord.
Vi blygdest
for å kalle henne
det ho var for oss.

Vi sveitta inderleg
i sola der.
Jorda sa til oss i brorskap:
Du og eg—
Vi vann ikkje svara.

A Word in the Fall

Then it came to September.
Became glowing September.
Still and clear between the mountains,
and clear overhead.

Huge clear spaces were out wandering,
and inside
September's bell called us
to the toil of labor.

We went to the earth.
To everyone's earth.
We were shy of calling her
what she was for us.

There in the sun we sweated bullets.
The earth said to us in brotherhood:
You and I—
We couldn't answer.

Seint i tunet

Mørk, med skodd og regn
har septemberkvelden vori,
og ljosrunden i tunet har stridd for livet
og har i avmakt sett grensa straks her borte,
så ein no står som inni ei rom røvarhole
frå ei barndomsbok.

Aldri blir dette anna det kjende tunet
i glinsande gras-skimmer for ein seint heimkomen,
og innramma av huslengder som ein knapt ser
i denne stund, men veit alt om.
Tunge som aningar er husa no,
dei som elles er så venlege av tre.

Godt er å sova bak tre.
Ein står i eit vått tun og veit kva ein seier.
Ingen ljod kan høyrast frå noken kant,
for inni her søv det utan botn.
Barn og vaksne ligg drukna
i haustens sommarmette svevn.

Late, in the Yard

It's been dark, with mist and rain,
this September evening,
and the circle of light in the yard has struggled for life
and finally settled for borders right here,
so now you're standing as if in a big robber's camp
from a book in your childhood.

This will never be anything but the familiar yard
glistening with a shimmer of grass for a late homecoming,
and framed by long housefronts that you barely see
at this hour, but know everything about.
They're heavy as premonitions now,
these houses that in daylight are friendly wood.

It's best to sleep behind wood.
You're standing in a wet yard and know what you're talking about.
No sound can be heard from anywhere,
for in here sleep is bottomless.
Children and grown-ups lie drowned
in the summer-sated sleep of autumn.

Mellom blå skuggar

Høge ospetre,
men ikkje ei rørsle
i eit skapt lauv
—så stille er det blivi.
Og småbuskane
vågar ikkje for sitt liv
røre på seg,
når store bror
some sildrar oppi himmelen
heller ikkje torer eller kan.

Så stille er det blivi.
Og her omsider
er mennesket hamna,
sviande
av eit vondt ord
så skarpt i kanten
som eit hogg,
eller som fjellrender i vest
etter solarglad,
—slik dei er just no.

Langt borte er du, duvande eng!
full av rik forvirring
—ikkje tenk på henne.
Her dalar blå skuggar ned
så fuglar teier.
Dalar ned med ro.
Ein veit ikkje lenger,
iblant alt dette,
om det tyder noko
det som var vondt—

Between Blue Shadows

Tall aspens,
but not a stir
in a single leaf
—it's grown so still.
And the small bushes
won't dare
make a move,
when the big fellows
that ripple up in the sky
don't dare to either, or can't.

It's grown so still.
And here's where you've
finally landed,
smarting
from a painful word
sharp-edged
as an axe,
or as mountain ridges to the west
in the glow of dusk
—the way they are right now.

You're far away, swaying meadow!
full of rich confusion
—don't think about her.
Here blue shadows settle down
so birds fall silent.
Settle down calmly.
You no longer know,
amid all this,
if what hurt
still matters—

Du og eg heilt stille

Som ein regnverskveld
i ein skinsommar—

Dei forbrende marikåpene
blir langsamt kalla til liv
ved det som skjer no.

Himmel og jord—
kva er det eine og kva er det andre?
Den eine har fullt av den andre i seg
i ein slik time,
ved slikt strøymande av godt.

Ein ange som ein ikkje har lært om
i alle sine lære-år
—no er han her
like ved mitt kinn.
Og medan den våte skuminga aukar
blir vegene i vatnet utydelege,
som til å gå på når alt er slutt,
og trea ved stranda er ikkje tre
men du og eg heilt stille,
og stranda er inga strand
eller grense meir.

You and I Completely Still

Like a rainy evening
in a long summer of drought—

The parched lady's-mantle
is slowly called to life
by what is happening now.

Heaven and earth—
what is the one and what is the other?
One is entirely full of the other
at such an hour,
in such a flood of well-being.

A fragrance one never learned about
in all one's years of study
—now it's here
right beside my cheek.
And as the damp twilight deepens
the paths in the lake grow unclear,
as if for walking on when everything's over,
and the trees near the shore are not trees
but you and I completely still,
and the shoreline is no line
or boundary anymore.

Død sjø

Det var ein sjø
her, før,
med alle dovne bylgjer
varme av sol
kring vakre kne.
Ein var i det.

Sjå den is-sletta
no i dag
utan eit levande punkt.
Det er eg som står slik
på stranda.
Ser—

Ingen hindrar meg å fara,
langt bort.
Det brest av aukande kjøld
i stive flater
og i stive sinn.
Eg blir for det, her.

Det som skræmer,
mest av alt,
er steinskallane i stranda.
Stumme klagarar,
ein halv fot opp av isen,
—som drukna seidmenn.

Men det som bind
bind,
er den trassige vona
på omslag:
Varme.
Nye bårer.

Dead Lake

There was a lake here before,
all sun-warmed lazy waves
around pretty knees.
We were part of this.

Look at the plain of ice now
without one point of life.
I'm the one standing here
on the beach.
I look—

There's no one to stop me from leaving this
far behind.
Deepening cold is cracking
stiff surfaces
and stiff lives.
Even so, I'll stay here.

What terrifies
most of all,
is the stone skulls in the beach.
Mute grievers,
a half-foot out of the ice,
—like drowned shamans.

But what forms
attachments,
is the obstinate hope
for change:
Warmth.
New breakers.

Ute susar vinden

Ute susar vinden
lågt igjennom mørkret,
lågt igjennom trea
ingen lenger ser—
Lågt frå opne hjarte
stig det enkle ordet
om at du og eg
har enn einannen kjær.

Denne låge vindrøyst
ifrå ingen stader
blandar seg med dine
sakte sagde ting—
Famnen din er open.
Handa di er venleg.
Natta sveiper tett
sitt store teppe kring.

Høyr kor svevntungt lauvet
utpå kvisten raslar—
sommaren igjennom
har det levt sitt liv.
Men i denne natta
hausten kjem med stormen
og det veike bladet
ned av kvisten riv.

Aningar om stormen,
om den tunge skaking,
er det vel som fører
deg og meg i hop.
Aningar om einsemd,
om ein frost som sniker,
om eit fall som trugar,
om eit fåfengt rop.—

Outside the Wind Whispers

Outside the wind
whispers through the dark,
softly, through trees
no one can see now—
Softly, from open hearts
the simple word floats up:
that you and I, love,
are still each other's.

This low voice
of wind from nowhere
blends itself
with your slowly spoken words—
Your body is open.
Your hand is friendly.
The night wraps us tight
in its giant quilt.

Hear how the branches are rustling
and sighing, heavy with sleep—
they've lived their life
for the whole summer.
But fall will come
with the storm tonight
and strip off
the weakened leaves.

Inklings of the storm,
of the heavy trembling,
are surely what drive
us together.
Inklings of loneliness,
of a creeping frost,
an imminent fall,
a futile cry.—

Dersom mørkrets teppe
lyftest brått bort av deg,
fekk eg kanskje skode
meir enn eg veit om:
At du midt i heten
sansar såre varsel,
søker angst eit feste
i det vide rom.

If the dark's quilt
suddenly lifts from you
perhaps I will see
more than I could guess:
That in the midst of the heat
you sense a painful warning,
search, frightened, for a
grip in the wide space.

Lenger og lenger bort
(Til ein diktar)

No ser vi huset.—
Stumt bulnar det fram
or regnversluft og kveld.

Og dine tre—
dine unge sovande tre.
Og du sjølv. Din urolege svevn.

Din djupe drikk
av kjærleiks kjelde her
har førebudd alt omkring deg.

Her går få inn.
Men det ditt hjarta elskar står her,
så her er mangment ute.

Møt din fred med ro.
Ditt bu er oppgjort om våren.
Langt unna går fuglane ein stad,

—for å tala om dei.
Men helst talar vi om eit menneske
som skjøna andre menneskes naud.

Imedan kverv huset ditt
lenger og lenger inn i kvelden,
i regnluft og fugletrekk utom tid.

Farther and Farther Away
(To a Writer)

Now we see the house—
silently emerging from
evening and air that smells of rain.

And your trees—
your young, sleeping trees.
And you yourself. Your uneasy sleep.

You drew deep here
from the well of love,
nurtured everything around you.

Few enter.
But what your heart loved is still here,
so that many stand outside.

Rest easy.
Your legacy will be ours in the spring.
The birds are somewhere far away,

—if we're to speak of them.
But we'd rather speak of a man
who understood other people's despair.

Meanwhile your house swirls further and further
into the evening, into rain-filled
air and the passage of birds beyond time.

Køyrekaren

Ute:
ein brå ljod i kulden
frå lange tømmerlass
i tung fart ned bakken
forbi huset og så bort.

Men det var ein full tone.
Trestammer song
mot hardfrosen veg.
Ein full song om vinter
og mannsarbeid.

Inne er stilt nok:
Siste minutten i livet
for ein gamal farar på tømmervegen.
Fort går minstevisaren på klokka
frå strek til strek.

Små sekundar—
Han skimtar kvinna si i skodd no
og prøvar gripa noko av det.
Han vil minnast.
Men underet grånar i handa.
Det er lenge sidan regnbogens tid.

Då syng det opp der ute.—
Helsar han til
frå hans eiga verd.
Lange tunge lass.
Hans eigen manndoms song
i strenge vintrar.

The Logger

Outside:
a sharp sound in the cold
from long loads of timber
moving heavily downhill
past the house and then away.

But it was a full note.
Tree-trunks sang
against frozen road.
A full song about winter
and men's work.

Inside it's quiet enough:
The last minute of life
for an old traveler on the logging road.
The second-hand on the clock moves fast
from line to line.

Small seconds—
He glimpses his woman in a mist now
and tries to catch hold.
He wants to remember.
But the vision fades to gray.
It's a long time since the rainbow years.

Then a song rises outside—
salutes him
from his own world.
Long heavy loads.
The song of his manhood
in hard winters.

Lynet

Lynet ligg ferdig bak svarte skyer,
i brå kvævande stille,
med sin logande orm
klar til å renne i jorda.
Ingen som det i ålvor fór til hjarta
har hatt mæle å fortalt med sidan.
Den blinde strålen råka berre:
det var å døy einsam frå.

— —

Lyn ligg ferdig om så skyer aldri finst,
innpakka i eld i blå luft, i ein tanke,
nedlagt i ei kvitnande sanning
som alltid har funnist,
gøymt, med sine guddommelege kvister
alltid ferdige til ljosbliving
grunnleggande jordskaking
og veldig utbreiing.

Så maktlaust som lynet frå skya blir
med sine blinde slag.

The Lightning

Lightning waits behind black clouds,
in sharp smothering silence,
its blazing snake
ready to run the earth through.
No one whom it's wounded to the heart
had voice to speak of it later.
The blind flash just struck:
made you die alone and leave things.

—— —

Lightning waits even without clouds,
packed in fire in blue air, in a thought,
stored in a whitening truth
that's always been there,
hidden, with its divine branches
always ready for the change to light,
the transfiguring earthquake,
enormous expansion.

The lightning from clouds seems so powerless
with its blind bolts.

Regn i Hiroshima

I det ho lyfte handa
for å ta tekanna
kom eit blindande ljos—

var ikkje meir
alt var borte
dei var borte
omlaga til damp og sky,
gåtefullt, oppstigande og stumt.
Rop var ikkje rop i dette.
Men jorda slo høgt og vilt
ein knyttneve mot himmelen
ved mishandling,
—ved det attlevande veit
verda rundt
men ikkje orkar fatte:
Hiroshima—

Stigande milevide slør,
dei var i det,
gått attende til ei urform.
Ein skjerm av damp
over ei pint jord.
Vera eit grann av dette.

Vera i det bortdragande—
Men ikkje lenge.
Det drog snart meir frå kaos.
Sløret vart dropar tett i tett,
i dropens evige skapnad
utan byrjing eller slutt.

Dei fall,
svalande, utalde,
i tungt regn nedover—

Rain in Hiroshima

As she lifted her hand
to reach for the teapot
there was a blinding light—

no more
everything was gone
they were gone
transformed to steam and cloud,
mysterious, ascending, and mute.
Cries weren't cries in this.
But wildly the earth thrust up
against the sky a clenched fist
at its abuse
—at what survivors know
around the world
but cannot grasp:
Hiroshima—

Rising mile-wide mist—
they were part of it—
gone back to a primordial form.
A veil of steam
above a tortured earth.
To be a particle of this.

To be part of what's driven off—
but not for long.
Soon chaos took in more.
The veil became drops packed tight,
in the eternal shape of drops
without beginning or end.

They fell,
cooling, uncounted,
downward in a heavy rain—

FRÅ

Lykka for ferdesmenn
1949

FROM

The Wanderer's Reward

1949

Der logen brann

Ved den lange grå vegen
er der oske etter utbrend eld
og merke av oppbrot
i dust og hete.

Det er alt.
Men logen som brann
i krinsen av dei reisande
kvarv berre for auga,
i usløkt trå.

Dei reiste for ein draum
og kunne gje alt,
og måtte lenger i si søking
og si uro,
og bålet brenn vidare
i alle synsrender,
medan nye søkarar grev i oska
og i grunnen under oska,
og draumen
er det som er lykka
for ferdesmenn.

Where the Fire Burned

Beside the long gray road:
the ashes of burned-out fires
and signs of departure
in dust and heat.

That's all.
But the fire that burned
in the circle of wanderers
faded only from sight,
its longing unquenched.

They wandered for a dream,
could give without limit
and had to go further, searching
and restless,
and the blaze keeps burning
on every horizon,
while new seekers dig in the ashes
and in the ground under the ashes,
and it's the dream that is
the wanderer's reward.

Ormens veg over berget

Det solvermde berget
har slette linne kuv
og heite skrånande sider
—ingen går der for sitt liv.

Ingen har møtt noken.
Aldri var der spor i steinen.
Aldri har lyngen rasla.
Berget skin av gru.

Som isande gliding
over ein heit barm—
men eit berg er stumt,
ikkje ropar eit berg ut noko
før dagen er der
då både berg og skyer skal rope.
Og ormen skrid over,
slipar langsamt berget
i sine gjeremål,
og fuglen som skal i suget
syng.

The Serpent's Way

The sun-warmed mountain
has smooth, gentle domes
and hot sloping sides
—no one dares to walk there.

No one has met anyone there.
The rock has never been scratched.
No heather has ever rustled.
The mountain shines with terror.

Like a shiver sliding
across a burned breast—
but a mountain is mute,
a mountain won't say a thing
until the day has come
when both mountain and clouds must cry out.
And the snake slips over,
slowly polishing the mountain
as it does its work,
and the bird that will be consumed
sings.

Dunder under is

Morgonside?
—dette er bortanfor
morgon og kveld.—
Vi vaknar berre og høyrer
at no går det, ute,
i si eiga dobbelte natt.
Det durar under isen
frå ei verd som ikkje er vår,
klumsande ladd
bak ein ljod.

Det gjeld nok oss,
men lite veit vi,
der vi krøkest som i morsliv
under teppet.

Vi høyrer med det store
rid i veg under isen,
blant svartgrøne berg av vår trass.
Grunnfeste berg i det rasande.
Glatthogne berg.
Framoverlutte berg,
slipa av forbifarande
helvets-ferder
i alle våre tider.

Booming under Ice

Towards morning?
—this is beyond
morning and evening.—
We just awaken and hear
that it's moving now, outside,
in its own double night.
Booming under the ice
from a world that is not ours—
it stuns, loaded
behind a sound.

Concerns us, all right,
but we don't know much,
as we curl into fetal position
under the blanket.

We listen as the great mass
rides on under the ice,
past the black-green cliffs of our defiance.
Anchored cliffs amid the ripping loose.
Cliffs ground smooth.
Overhanging cliffs,
polished by passing
expeditions to hell
through all our days.

Glasveggen

Mellom deg og meg
står ein ljodlaus vind
som ein glasvegg:
Det er glasveggens dag.

Kvar gong eg ser mot deg
opnar du munnen
og ropar,
men ikkje eit ord når gjennom.

Auga ditt vidar seg
og les på munnen min
at eg òg
ropar bittert.

Ja i slike stunder
pressar du andletet mot glaset
som eit vilt barn,
og blir vanskapt i draga av det.
Oppsvulna og forvrengd av ynske
ligg du mot på andre sida
og alt er stumt.

The Glass Wall

Between you and me
a soundless wind
stands like a glass wall:
The day of the glass wall has come.

Each time I look toward you
you open your mouth
and call,
but not a word gets through.

Your eyes widen
and read from my mouth
that I too
am calling bitterly.

Yes, at such moments
you press your face against the glass
like a frantic child,
and it deforms your features.
Swollen and twisted by wanting
you lie up against it on the other side
and muteness rules.

Slik var den draumen

— — —byrjinga
er ikkje her,
slutten
er løynd,
ingen stans i dette,
i straumen,
draget i sinnet
ved ting som er ugripelege,
ugripeleg
som angen av forbi-fari
morgonregn,
useieleg
som synet av vårsnø
over kvitveis,
veikt
som ein hug i einrom
og bittert
som orda umogeleg
og for seint,
og bittert
som tanken på
at no strekker du deg
framfor spegelen av
unemneleg sol
i din glans
som ingen skal skode.

And Then There Was the Dream

— — —the beginning
isn't here,
the end
is hidden,
no pause in this,
in the current,
the pull in the mind
from things that are impalpable,
impalpable
as the scent
of morning rain just ended,
ineffable
as the sight of spring snow
on white anemones,
weak
as a heart in private
and bitter
as the words impossible
and too late,
and bitter
as the thought
that you're stretching now
before the mirror of
unmentionable sun,
in your glory
that no one will see.

Det ror og ror

Dagen er faren
—og det ror og ror.

Det mørke berget,
mørkare enn kvelden,
luter over vatnet
med svarte folder:
Eit samanstupt andlet
med munnen i sjøen.
Ingen veit alt.

Der ror og ror,
i ring,
for berget syg.
Forvilla plask på djupet.
Forkoment knirk i tre.
Forvilla trufast sjel som ror
og snart kan sugast ned.

Han står der òg
den andre,
han i bergfoldene,
i svartare enn svart,
og lyer utover.
Lam av synd.
Stivt lyande.
Stiv av støkk
fordi her ror—

Då må det gå blaff og blå-skin
fram og attende
som heite vindar
og som frost.

Endlessly Rowing

The day has ended
—and there is a rowing without end.

The dark cliff,
darker than the evening,
leans its black creases
over the water:
A jackknifed face
with its mouth in the lake.
No one knows everything.

There is an endless rowing,
in circles,
for the mountain is sucking in.
Bewildered splashing on the deep.
Exhausted creaking of wood.
Bewildered, a faithful soul is rowing
and may soon be sucked down.

He too is standing there,
that other
in the creases of the cliff,
in the blacker than black,
and listening over the water.
Paralyzed by sin.
Stiffly listening.
Stiff with shock
because there is a rowing here—

Until a gust and a blue light jump
out and back
like hot winds
and like frost.

Det ror og ror i natt.
Det ser og ser ingen.
Ingen veit
kven som slikkar på berget
når det er mørkt.
Ingen veit botnane
i Angest sjø.
Ingen veit
kven som ikkje kan ro.

There is an endless rowing tonight.
There is an endless seeing by no one.
No one knows
who will be lapping at the mountain
when it's dark.
No one knows the levels
at the bottom of Lake Angst.
No one knows
who may not be rowing.

FRÅ

Løynde eldars land
1953

FROM

Land of Hidden Fires

1953

Båten ved land

Din stille båt
har ikkje namn.
Din stille båt
har ikkje hamn.
Din gøymde båt ved land.

For dette er då ikkje hamnen—
Lauvet blikar i vårnettene
oppover den ventande ferdige båten,
og drys gult og vått
nedover toftene i oktober,
og ingen har vori her.

Men her finst sòg ifrå endelause
sletter av sjø,
der soler går opp av djupet
og vinden går mot hamnen bakom.

Men det er heller ikkje hamnen,
anna ein stad med sòg og kalling
frå endå større sletter,
større storm i strendene,
og ein større båt om kvelden.

Din stille båt
gror langsamt ned.
Din gøymde båt ved land.

The Boat on Land

Your still boat
hasn't got a name.
Your still boat
hasn't got a port.
Your secret boat on land.

For this is no port—
On spring nights the leaves slosh white
above the ready, waiting boat,
and sprinkle down yellow and wet
onto the thwarts in October,
and no one has been here.

But there's a pull here from endless
plains of smooth sea,
where suns rise from the deep
and the wind blows toward the harbor beyond.

But that's not a port either—
rather a place with a pull, a calling
from still larger plains,
a larger storm along the shore,
and a larger boat in the evening.

Your still boat
is slowly overgrown.
Your secret boat on land.

Sporet

På den bortløynde sandstranda er
der ingen lenger.
Over står berga forbrende.

Ein sandboge, bittert forleten,
full av eit einaste spor! forleten,
fråflydd etter bresteferdig venting.

Over står berga forbrende.
Noken har vori her
og gått og gått
—men over *dette* vatnet kom det ingen.

Sanden var berre innramma av underlege berg.
Den gule sanden
med sine siste einsame spor.

Hastig samanrasa spor.
Tallause søkk i sanden berre.
Vandringa av din unge fot i vilske,
dine mjuke steg, i torste, før du flydde.
Din beste draum for ingen.
Din gylne skapnad bortspilt.
Herlege evner for ingen ingen
—medan dei svarte bergsidene stod over
med grimer i draga
frå tidlegare liv.

The Footprints

On the secluded beach
there's no one now.
The mountains above are scorched.

An arc of sand, bitterly abandoned,
covered by one person's tracks! abandoned,
deserted after a harrowing wait.

The mountains above are scorched.
Someone has been here
and paced and paced
—but no one came across *this* lake.

The sand was completely closed off by strange mountains.
The yellow sand
with its last, lonely tracks.

Hurried footprints, caved in.
Just countless depressions in the sand.
The trail of your young foot in a frenzy,
your soft steps, in thirst, before you fled.
Your best dream, for no one.
Your golden form, wasted.
Splendid powers, for no one, no one
—while the black cliffs looked on
with streaks down their features
from previous lives.

Huset på tvers

Punktet i natta
er eit stort hus
fullt av slæpande,
basta og bundi
til si tunge svill
—mykje skulle vi gje
for at ikkje det var til.

Alltid det huset på tvers.
Med tunge saker tenkt inn der.
Alt som i grunnen er *vårt*.
For det er vi som skulle vori der,
synest vi stadig.
Vi skulle teki børene
og sveitten.

Som skuldmenn går vi framom
fordi vårt liv vart lettare.
Det svarte punktet ligg der og blir mørkare.
Huset der dei slit med
det vi skulle sliti.
Der *vi* har det opnande ordet.
Men ordet har vi kasta i ein brunn.

Framom så hastig.
Vi veit det så tydeleg
alt som går for seg
og auga slår vi ned:
Kjøvande luft der. Strimer i andletet.
Dødtrøytt svevn der
med sin gløymsel.

Framom der endå ein gong.
Skjert anar vi vår vanmakt.
Mykje skulle vi bytte av tida vår
imot kraft og kjærleik.

The Skewed House

The point in the night
is a large house
full of toil,
lashed to its heavy
foundation of timbers
—how we wish
it didn't exist.

Always that skewed house.
With heavy thoughts read into it.
Everything that's really *ours*.
Because it should have been us there,
we keep thinking.
We should have accepted the burden
and the sweat.

We walk past like debtors
because our life turned out easier.
The black point stands there, growing darker.
The house where they've sweated at
toil that should have been ours.
Where *we* had the password.
But we dropped the word down a well.

Walk past so quickly.
We understand clearly
everything that's going on
and we lower our eyes:
Stifling air inside. Streaked faces.
Exhausted sleep in there
and its oblivion.

Walk past one more time.
We shrink in our weakness.
We would trade a good deal of our time
for strength and love.

Mykje skulle vi gje av tid
for å orke seia ordet.
Men ordet ligg på botnen av ein brunn.

We would give a good deal of time
to be able to say the word.
But the word is at the bottom of a well.

Vi fyller dei vidaste nettene

Glatt er glasberget:
eit sjølvlysande berg om kvelden,
eit glinsande berg av heilskap,
i dei underlege nettene
nede ved foten av det,
der *vi* er.

Her alt er alt, kan du
ikkje vera lenge,
du som er samansett av halvt og ulikt,
og menneske av kjøt og veikskap
—her er det inga forståing.
Men det seier i deg: eg vil.
Det seier oppatt og utruleg at eg vil.

Tallause er vi
alle som vil vera her.
Alle som vil
trass alt vi gjer.
Vi fyller dei vidaste nettene.
Og vårt ørvesle sjølvlysande grann
blir samanlagt som ei ljosskodd
lågt nede ved marka
—ved det store berget
der inga forståing finst.

We Fill the Widest Nights

How slippery the mountain of glass:
an iridescent mountain in the evening,
a glittering mountain of wholeness,
in the mysterious nights
down at its foot
where *we* are.

Here where everything is whole
you can't stay long,
made as you are by halves, of hybrid stuff,
human with weakness
—here there is no understanding.
But something inside you says: I want to.
Says again, incredibly: I want to.

We are countless,
we who want to stay here.
Who want to
in spite of everything we do.
We fill the widest nights.
And our tiny iridescent particles
are fused into a luminous mist
lying just above the ground
—beside the great mountain
where there is no understanding.

Skuggane på neset

Svarte skuggar sig om nes utan opphald
og utan ljod,
for slik er det i vår hug.

Slik samlast vi på neset
etter som dagen minkar.
Og etter som ljoset minkar
står vi alt stillare,
utan å fortelje grunnen.
Stillare og stillare
på våre nes.

Det vart ein heit dag
å koma igjennom,
kunne vi sagt.
Ein logande dag.
Men vi teier.

Vi kjenner berre dagen som ein slokna klang.
No kjenner vi kvelden, lang og forunderleg.
Varme steinar etter brennande sol
som no er borte.
Dirrande aningar og sjølvlysande minne.
Nedtrakka blomar og knuste bilete,
og såre kne.
Alt det vi ikkje ville gjort
gjorde vi sju gonger.
Så var det slutt.

Men her på neset kan vi ikkje vera
for det—
Vi står her berre, ventar noko nytt.
Ved alle brende nes glid elvar,

Shadows on the Point

Black shadows slide around the point with no let-up
and without a sound,
for that's what it's like in our minds.

That's how we've gathered at the point
as the day ebbs.
And as the light ebbs
we stand all the more still,
without saying why.
Stiller and stiller
on our point.

It turned into a hot day
to get through,
we might have said.
A burning day.
But we're silent.

We feel the day only as a muted ringing.
Now we feel the evening, long and mysterious.
Stones warmed by flaming sun
that's gone now.
Trembling premonitions and luminous memories.
Trampled flowers and broken pictures,
and sore knees.
Everything we wouldn't have wanted done
we did ten times over.
Then it was finished.

But at any rate we can't stay here
on the point—
We're just standing here waiting for something new.
Rivers go drifting past every scorched point,

og på neset står skuggane og blygest,
og ventar båten.
Den årelause båten er vår lodd.
All styring teken frå oss.

Vi står her i di djupe natt, Natt,
og ventar det nye bak odden.
Straumen går svart og stille.
Og det vi kjenner ved det
fortel vi ikkje til einannen.

and on the point the shadows stand ashamed
and wait for the boat.
The oarless boat is our fate.
All steering taken from us.

We stand here in your deep night, Night,
and wait for something new from beyond the point.
The current runs black and silent.
And what we feel through it
we don't tell each other.

Hete

Dei kjære aldri nemner det.
Men andre seier: her stod eg,
det var ein fredag,
og akkurat her—

Kring heile grannelaget femner det:
Minnest det var fredag,
minnest etter frostnetter
minnest etter tele,
marka hard over indre ukjent
—i dette kunne det koma
utan varsel, og det kom:
Utan vidare revna her i underlege mønster,
braut fram glødande sidan lange tider,
skok dei støaste, sette i brann ikring seg,
slutta ikkje før alt var uttømt,
øydde seg sjølv, og mørkna
—var ikkje jordlag og tele,
var ein venleg daglegdags mann.

Hans kjære var hans kjære til han brann.
Grannelaget kjende han:
Hans ro. Hans enkle tale.
Hans tagalle strenge liv
med veike gøymde søkk i, kjende få.
Nettene var hans eigne, og unemnde av soga.
Slagghaugar i lendet:
Halvgløymde utbrot.
Livlause rester
og samstundes minning
om dei løynde eldanes land.
Her er det meste bak skalet,
her må det koma som utbrot,
her må dei tære seg sjølve
med underjords hete og vald.

Heat

His loved ones never mention it.
But others say: here's where I was standing,
it was a Friday,
and right here—

Circling the neighborhood:
I remember it was Friday,
after the night frosts, I remember,
after the freeze, I remember,
the fields hard above unknown interiors
—a time when it could come
without warning, and it came:
Suddenly cracked in strange patterns,
erupted, red hot since long before,
shook the steadiest, sent flames all around,
didn't stop until everything was spent,
destroyed itself, and grew dark
—was no longer a layer of frozen soil and earth,
was a friendly, ordinary man.

His loved ones were his loved ones till he burned.
The neighbors knew him:
His calm. His simple speech.
But his strict and silent life,
full of weak, hidden pores, was known to few.
The nights were his own, not part of the story.
Hills of cinder in the terrain:
Half-forgotten eruptions.
Lifeless remains
and at the same time reminders
of the land of hidden fires.
Here almost everything's under a shell,
it's got to break out in eruptions;
here they've got to consume themselves
in underground heat and violence.

Men varsel fekk dei, om det store, dei han drogst til.
No etterpå skjønar dei det var fullbyrding, alt.
Auga hans lengta mot fullbyrding—
veit dei no.
Dei *venta* det frigjorde ropet frå han,
og var sjølve ferdige å møte
—slik òg han visste *det*
og hadde sine mot-rop klar
—slik farleg vekselspel blir planlagt.
Og når skuggen er større enn slagghaugar, revnar det.
Når vona om løysing er lengst borte, revnar det.
Ein frostmorgon revna det ikringom,
og alt innom synsvidd vart vitne
med elden frå under kom naken.

Lufta vart næring, rasande næring,
sugande nedi
og inn.
Revnene kom undantil,
rann bortover som ormar,
auka seg og sprengde
—midt i det kom grunn-duren,
opna sine sluser,
så kvar som stod her høyrde
stod klumsa i sitt indre,
kvar som var vitne, kjende skuld.

Han brann, og ropte i sin vande, si frigjering.
Revnene vart gap. Sundsprengde frostkantar.
Fullt fullt av frigjort!
Elden som lufta trekte sugande ned mot,
røyk som dreiv bort då logen vart heitare,
så allting låg opent som det *er*
mellom menneske.
Han ropte sine rop i lette,
om det som hadde brunni

But they were warned of the crisis, the ones he was drawn to.
Now they understand it was all a fulfillment.
His eyes yearned for fulfillment—
they know this now.
They *expected* a cry of release from him,
and were themselves prepared to meet it
—just as he knew *this*
and had his countercries ready
—dangerous volleys are planned.
And when the shadow is bigger than hills of cinder, cracks come.
When hope of solutions is far off, cracks come.
One frosty morning the cracks were all around,
and everything within sight bore witness
as the fire from below arrived naked.

The air became its food, raging food,
sucked downward
and in.
The cracks came from underneath,
ran outward like snakes,
widened and burst
—while the ground thundered,
opened its floodgates,
so each person who heard
stood spellbound to his core,
each person who witnessed it
knew guilt.

He burned, and called out in his distress, his liberation.
The cracks became chasms. Blasted rims of frost.
Wholly liberated!
Fire that suctioned the air down into it,
smoke that drifted away when the blaze grew hotter,
so everything lay open, as it *is*
between people.
He called out his cries in relief,
they spoke of what had burned

utan luft.
Underleg var det, hjelpelaust og vågsamt:
Rop som ingen forstod mellom braka,
andres uskjønlege svar attende,
og som hans eigne førebudde mot-rop slo i svime,
ord som ingen ville skjøna, om det så var stilt.

Tett tett innpå var dei kjære,
for å mildne, for å stenge,
bli herre over utbrotet
—i røynsle etter småutbrot frå før.
Men dette skok frå djupare enn der dei var,
frå der ingen kan skjøne eller mildne.
Sjå fekk dei òg at han ikkje prøvde sløkke,
såg at han ville det, det løyste dei frå redsla,
det er vi! ropte dei endå, til fånyttes i larmen,
og mot glødande floder av underjord.
Til fånyttes i larmen,
men dei såg dei var hans eigne
heile tida, der krateret brann reint.
—Medan andre, som også var støkt no og trong fred:
venlege han hadde vendt seg til,
fått hjelp av i sin veikskap,
brått utakksamt lagdest øyde, vart trekt inni
og strauk med.
Det er vi! sa òg slike, hemmelege, hjelparar,
i all sin rett,
men retten forkomst,
ingen såg dei,
deira små hus sveid av.

Han stod der og fylte sine tunge ord,
uskjønlege ord, og brann.
Å, stive mørke novemberring av vitne:
slik er elden.
Natt vart det ikkje om dagen lakka,
det lyste frå lånte kjelder
så lenge dette mennesket varde.

without air.
They were strange, helpless, risky:
Cries that no one took in amid the crashing noise,
amid the others' incomprehensible answers
sent spinning by his prepared echo-cries,
words no one would have understood,
even in silence.

His loved ones got so close to him,
to soothe, contain,
to master the eruption
—smaller ones had taught them how.
But this one shook from much deeper beneath them,
from a place where no one can soothe or understand.
And they saw he wasn't trying to taper off,
that he wanted this, and were released from their fear:
It's us! they even cried, uselessly amid the noise,
cried out to glowing floods of underworld.
Uselessly amid the noise,
but they saw they were his own people
the whole while, as the crater burnt out.
—While others, who also were scared now and craved peace,
friends he had turned to,
gotten help from in his weakness,
were ungratefully laid waste, pulled in,
and destroyed.
It's us! these said too, the hidden ones, the helpers,
as was their right,
but right was overcome,
no one saw them,
their small houses were set ablaze.

He stood there encompassed by his heavy words,
incomprehensible words, and burned.
O, stiff dark November ring of witnesses:
such is the fire.
Night did not fall if day waned,
light shone from borrowed sources
as long as he lasted.

Vara altfor lenge slapp det i si fullbyrdingstrå:
Ropinga av viktige bodskap vart dauvare,
duren i grunnen veikna og vart borte
og heten svalna seg i vinden.
Hans kjære stod fast på sine postar,
kjende seg ikkje knuste, men lyfte
—der eldberget kjøltest og stilna,
mørkna i fred til ein slagghaug.

Before too long, the yearning for fulfillment eased:
The cry of important messages grew fainter,
the rumbling of the ground weakened and vanished
and the heat cooled off in the wind.
His loved ones stood fast at their posts,
felt they were not crushed, but uplifted
—as the mountain of fire cooled and quieted down,
calmly became a dark hill of cinder.

FRÅ

Ver ny, vår draum

1956

FROM

Be New, Dream of Ours
1956

Båten

Glade let vi det mørkne litt
innan vi fór.
Og då vi kom utpå vart vi trolla
og gjorde venlege
av kvite hissige små-bårer mot neset,
på tvers av kolsvart vatn.
Som ein frasande festkjole
kring eit kne.

Vi lydde på frasinga
og blømde opp.
Men då vi kom lenger ut
vart vi støkte
og tenkte ikkje meir så lett på kjolar:
Vi merkte ein stor puls
opp or dødens djup.

Andlet skifte farge kvar med seg.
Det vart ropt i dimma.
Men kvart namn som fanst
svara støkt frå båten,
at dei var med.

Etter det
var det havet.
Pulsen og havet.

The Boat

Happy, we let it grow darker
before we left.
And when we got out there
we felt friendly: enchanted by
eager white breakers near the point,
they cut across the coal-black water
like a party dress swishing
around a knee.

We listened to the rushing
and livened up.
But when we got further out
we grew frightened
and didn't think so readily of dresses:
We felt a great pulse
coming up from Death below.

Each face changed color in its own way.
A call sounded in the dusk.
But all the names
answered frightened from the boat
that they were there.

After that
there was the ocean.
The pulse and the ocean.

Ein namnlaus ring i veden

Du spurde før det skjedde:
kvar er *mitt* tre blant tre?
Ingen svara.
Fleire spørsmål vart det ikkje tid til.
Klokka ringde.
Brått skjedde tinga
der du gjekk og stod.

Sterk saft veld opp i mengd
bak borkens grove hud.
Ein fugl sit vakt
og allting er i orden.

Du er ein del av dette,
som du visste,
der du gjekk avstengd frå det
med din draum,
men dine tyrste stille drag av sakn,
der dine røter var og er og blir.

Så er det timen. Alt frå før er gløymt:
For du blir lett på handa, utan varsel
—og det er du, som var så tung i grepet.
Det lykkas for deg. Du får ynsket oppfylt.
Lykkas, lykkas.
Alt du rører
formar seg og lykkas, to sekund.
Ingen ser det. Ingen skjønar
at det er det siste,
før det er skjedd.
Då skjønar heller ingen.

No er det slutt.
Men treet det var ditt.
Det går sin gang bak borken.
Du med di unge saft blir denne år-ring,

A Nameless Ring in the Wood

You asked before it happened:
where is *my* tree among trees?
No one answered.
There was no time for more questions.
The clock chimed.
Suddenly things happened to you
when you were unprepared.

Strong juice welled up in force
under the bark's rough skin.
A bird keeps watch
and everything's in its place.

You are a part of this,
which you knew
even as you lived shut off from it—
with your dream,
with your quiet, thirsting aspect of loss—
where your roots were, and are, and remain.

Then it's time. The past is forgotten:
For you grow light-handed, without warning
—you, who had such a firm grip.
You succeed. Your wish is fulfilled.
Succeed, succeed.
Everything you touch
takes form and succeeds, for two seconds.
No one sees it. No one understands
that this is the last thing
until it's happened.
No one understands it then, either.

Now it's over.
But the tree was yours.
Life takes its course under the bark.
You with your young sap become this ring,

som hardnar seg til ved og leikar leiken.
Ditt unge døds-år blir ein ring i veden.
Når treet veks seg fjernt og stort mot himlen
og brusar gjennom midnatt med sin styrke,
då er du midt i veden mellom mange.
Din ring er din og lever dine liv.

which hardens into wood and plays its role.
Your young dying year becomes a ring in the wood.
When the tree grows tall and broad against the sky
and sweeps through midnight with its strength,
then you are one among many in the wood.
Your ring is yours and lives your lives.

FRÅ

Liv ved straumen
1970

FROM

Life at the Stream
1970

Dei små gnagarane

Det knakar i stavane
i ein nedsnødd skigard.
Fonna tung som ein verden.
Men der er andre ting
å koma i hug:
Det svære snøpresset bryt sakte
og lydlaust inn
brystkorgene hos små gnagarar
nede på den marka ein ikkje lenger ser.
Alle som ikkje rakk å koma i livd
då snøveret sette i gang og gravla dei,
der dei gjekk og stod.

Alle små gnagarar
ligg mellom blakke våte strå
frå i sommar
og veit ingen ting om kvar dei er,
eller kva som er skjedd.
Tirande svarte auge pressa opne
ned i våte strå.
Vidt opne imot stormen.

Kviler i fred til våren.
Til våren
skal ein eller annan fugl finne dei,
hakke litt redd i dei,
ta dei i nebbet,
lyfte på dei, og vrake dei.

The Small Rodents

The rails are creaking
in a fence buried by snow.
The drift as heavy as a world.
But there are other things
to remember:
The huge weight of snow is slowly
and silently crushing
the rib cages of small rodents
down on the field you can no longer see.
The ones that didn't make it to shelter
when the snowstorm started and
buried them in their tracks.

The small rodents
lie amid pale wet grass
from the summer
and know nothing about where they are,
or what has happened.
Gleaming black eyes forced open
down in the wet grass.
Wide open, facing the storm.

They rest in peace till spring.
In the spring
some bird will find them,
peck at them warily,
take them in its beak,
lift them up, and discard them.

Sol-krå

Heime er ei sol-krå
der våren rører seg stille.
Dropar tiplar heile dagen.
Blanke dropar frå snøkanten,
dei speglar godt og vondt
i sitt korte fall, og knusest.
Sola er ein heit foss.

Der i sol-kråa,
der ein er født,
det er dropane her ein skulle
speglast i, og få på leppene,
skire frå snøkanten og
rett i hjartet.

Det er i den veike lukten
av vårvæte ein skulle sovne.
Det ropet ein skulle lyde.
Der ville det kjennast rett, alt.

Ut for bakke går det heile.
Alt er i sig mot eit fjernt mål,
alt er på veg til havet.
Eit ukjent hav inne i ein draum.
Alt av vårens sorg skal dit.
Alle tankar krinsar der
og blir sidan borte.

I sin barndoms sol-krå
sit ein når det ropar.

Sun-corner

At home there's a sun-corner
where spring quietly stirs.
Dripping all day long.
Clear drops from the snow-rim,
they reflect both good and bad
in their brief fall, and are shattered.
The sun is a hot cataract.

In that sun-corner,
where you were born—
it's those drops that should
mirror you, and wet your lips,
pure from the snow-rim and
right into your heart.

It's in that faint smell of
spring moisture you should fall asleep.
That call you should heed.
There, everything would feel right.

It's all moving downhill.
Everything's oozing toward a distant goal,
on its way to the sea.
An unknown sea inside a dream.
All of spring's sorrow is heading there.
All thoughts spiral there
and then disappear.

Your childhood sun-corner is where
you are when the call sounds.

Båten og fisken

Båten glid fram og lagar
ei mørk stripe på den grunne sanden.
Fisken ser opp i båtbotnen
og smiler det han er god for.
Kva trur den dumme båten?
Heile mitt liv har eg sett
den dumme båten koma.
Den tifald dumme båten
som vil fange meg.
Eg er lut lei han.

Smilet har fisken
i halen.
Med eit par smilande slag
er han borte.
Han ler lenge
bak ein brun stein.

The Boat and the Fish

The boat glides forward and makes
a dark stripe on the shallow sand.
The fish looks up at the keel of the boat
and smiles for all he's worth.
What is that stupid boat thinking?
All my life I've seen
that stupid boat coming.
That gigantically stupid boat
that wants to catch me.
I'm sick and tired of him.

A fish smiles
with its tail.
With a couple of smiling flips
he's gone.
He laughs for a long time
behind a brown rock.

Liv ved straumen

1

Vatnet trenger seg inn i strendene
saman med sola, gjennom tynne piper.
Det blir eit myrland for skyer av mygg.
Eit menneske kan bli rasande inni skya
og gå berserk-gang
med høge rop i mørkret.
Ikkje for myggens skuld,
men for det andre:
For det han kjenner
og ikkje kan forklare.

2

Fiskar mellom steinane
vippar med halen.
Dei veit ein god del om det som skjer.
Gamle fiskar med store hovud
kunne få eit menneske til å fryse
om dei fortalde.
Det blir aldri gjort.
Kjakane er samanbitne
og auga kalde.

3

I storr-graset ligg fuglar
med store, varme hjarte
bak dunen ein kveld,
med eit lågt sarr i storren.
Ein orm ligg natt etter natt og ventar
og får si løn.
Ingen veit meir, men den vesle fisken såg det.
Blodig og stum ligg kanskje fisken no
på fiskarens krakk.

Life at the Stream

1

The water forces its way into the banks
together with the sun, through thin channels.
They make a marshy home for clouds of mosquitoes.
A person can start raging inside the clouds
and go berserk,
crying loudly in the darkness.
Not because of the insects
but because of something else:
what he senses
and cannot explain.

2

Fish between the rocks
flip their tails.
They know a good deal about whatever happens.
Old fish with large heads
could make a person freeze
if they told all.
It will never happen.
Their jaws are clamped shut
and their eyes cold.

3

In the evening, in the sedge grass,
lie fowl with large, warm hearts
under their down, a low
murmur in the sedge.
A snake lies waiting night after night
and gets his reward.
No one knows, but the little fish saw it.
Perhaps the fish is lying bloody and silent now
on the fisherman's block.

4

Herlege sløkekroner svirrar
med frøhjul og godlukt.
Ved rota ligg eit menneske
og ein orm. Tiltrekte?
Det truskuldige mennesket
møter orm-auget i eit eldglimt.
Forståing spring imellom, og støkk.
Er det mogeleg!
Kven er eg?

5

Straumen har si sterke dragkraft.
Menneske legg seg i storr-graset
av uklare grunnar.
Redde og modige og gråtande.
Marka under dei er rå og duld.
Pusten frå straumen kjennest
som eit rop,
og menneske-hjartet skjelv og svarar.
Eg er på plass, svarar hjartet. Eg er med.

6

I sumplandet står
seige planter
med strålande fargar
og eit krumt fang.
Der syg dei livet av krek og fluger,
fangar føde med leik og slim-trådar.
Mennesket rykker seg ved synet,
synest at her
må helvetet vera nær.
Hit går mennesket
ikkje meir.

4

Magnificent angelica blossoms
are aswirl with seed-wheels and fragrance.
At their roots lie a person
and a snake. Attracted?
The innocent person
meets the snake-eye in a flash.
Understanding jumps the gap and stuns.
Is it possible!
Who am I?

5

The stream has a strong undertow.
People lie down in the sedge grass
for reasons that remain unclear.
Frightened and brave and weeping.
The ground beneath them is damp and hidden.
The breath of the stream can be felt
as a call,
and the human heart trembles and answers.
I am at my station, answers the heart. Here I am.

6

In the swamps stand
tough plants
with brilliant colors
and a curving embrace.
There they suck the life out of bugs and flies,
trap food with lures and with threads of slime.
People shudder at the sight,
think this place
must be close to hell.
People don't come here
any more.

7

Himmelen dreg saman tjukke skyer
til eit trugande møte.
Dei høgste trea sopar i det.
Det stivna storr-graset kviskrar:
Kva *er* dette?
Det svarar rundt ikring:
Det er du.
Og lenge lenge er det
til morgondag.

7

The sky gathers thick clouds
into a threatening band.
The tallest trees sweep through it.
The stiffened sedge grass whispers:
What *is* this?
The answer from all around:
It is you.
And tomorrow
will be a long time coming.

Gjennom nakne greiner

Dei nakne mars-greinene
står tett inn til glaset.
Dei er ved å sige inn
i mars-mørkret.
Men enno er dei mjuke og synlege,
meir velskapte enn det kan seiast.

Før dei blir borte
er det enno tid å tenke på
kva dei har tydd for ein,
og kva dei stadig er.
Ein tenker liksom at ein
alltid har sett sitt liv gjennom
mjuke, nakne greiner,
og grove greiner med tjukk bork.
Samanfiltring av luft og liv
og alt som strøymer.

Det stille greineverket blir dimmare
kvar gong eg ser opp.
Det kviler i vennleg skyming.
Eg synest det slår ut inni meg
fordi eg alltid har vori glad i det.
Borte i natta blir det ikkje,
ein har det med seg i sin eigen svevn
og legg seg trygt.
Om ein så ikkje skal slå auga oppatt i morgon.
Det tenker ein ikkje på.

No er det borte,
og ein går til ro.
Mellom nakne greiner
har livet fullbyrda seg.
Alle kvister,
alle greiner,
er med i svevnen.

Through Naked Branches

The naked branches of March
are up close to the window.
They're about to sink away
into the March darkness.
But they are still supple and visible,
better formed than you can say.

Before they vanish
there is still time to think about
what they have meant to you,
and what they continue to be.
You think it's as if you
have always seen your life through
supple, naked branches,
and coarse branches with thick bark.
An entanglement of air and life
and everything that flows.

The still network of branches grows dimmer
each time I look up.
It's resting in friendly dusk.
I think it's spreading out inside me
because I have always loved it.
It does not disappear in the night,
you take it with you into your own sleep
and lie down secure.
What if you don't open your eyes tomorrow.
You don't think about that.

Now it is gone,
and you take your rest.
Life has fulfilled itself
among naked branches.
All twigs,
all branches,
are there   in your sleep.

Frå stogetrammen

Skuggane sig innover sletta
som kjølege rolege venner
etter ein steikande dag.

Vår hug er eit tagalt
skuggerike.
Og skuggane sig innover
med sine vennlege gåter
og si dimme bløming.

Dei første skuggespissane
når fram til
føtene våre.

Vi ser roleg opp:
Er du alt der,
min mørke blom.

From the Stoop

The shadows creep in across the clearing
like cool, quiet friends
after a burning day.

Our mind is a silent
kingdom of shadow.
And the shadows creep inward
with their friendly riddles
and their twilit blossoming.

The first shadow-tips
reach our feet.

We look up calmly:
Are you here already,
my dark flower.

Reisa

Vi dukka endeleg fram att
av natt-skodda.
Ingen kjende einannan no.
Sansen var mist på ferda.
Ingen spurde heller krevjande:
Kven er du?

Svara kunne vi ikkje,
vi hadde mist
namna våre.

Langt borte dundra det
frå eit ubendig hjarte
som stadig var i arbeid.
Vi lydde utan å skjønne.
Vi var komne
lenger enn langt.

Journey

We finally appeared again
out of the night-fog.
And no one recognized anyone.
Underway we'd forgotten how.
Nor did anyone demand:
Who are you?

We couldn't have answered,
we had lost
our names.

Far off there was thunder
from an iron heart
that was always at work.
We listened without understanding.
We had come
farther than far.

Fuglen

Fuglen stod ferdig
ved vegen og venta.

Fuglen var eit under.
Hans svære venge-fang
var gløymsle.
Takten i hans hjarteslag
var min.

Saman sigla vi
inn i ukjent.
Utan spørsmål.
Utan sorg.

The Bird

The bird stood ready
by the roadside and waited.

The bird was a miracle.
Its great wingspan
was oblivion.
The rhythm of its heartbeat
was mine.

Together we sailed
into the unknown.
Without questions.
Without sorrow.

Ei lita uro

Ei lita uro i den nærmast
milevide enga.
Eit barn er komi på vilske
i eit hav.
Vinden lyfter litt i
hårtoppane.
Lyse hårtoppar iblant hundekjeks
og vikke.
Så er det lenge borte att.

Barnet har mist dei fire leiene,
veit ikkje kvar det er.
Så fyk håret opp i lufta att
på ein annan kant.
Har barnet gått på fire
mellom orm og gnagarar?
Det ropar ikkje,
synest det går i den rare verda
frå før det vart født, og tør ikkje rope.
Ingen vil finne det før til slåtten
på ein heit høyversdag.

Barnet vil ikkje koma ut av enga.
Det vil døy i si blomster-seng
i stille forundring.
Lett som ei fjør vil det
til slutt legge seg i eit
vikke-kjørr
og ikkje tenke.

A Little Disturbance

A little disturbance in the almost
mile-wide meadow.
A child has lost its way
in an ocean.
The wind fluffs
its hair.
Blond hair amid wild chervil
and vetch.
Then it's gone again for a long while.

The child has lost its bearings,
doesn't know where it is.
Then the hair blazes up again
at another spot.
Has the child crawled on all fours
among the snakes and rodents?
It doesn't cry out,
thinks it's moving in that strange world
it was in before it was born,
and doesn't dare to cry out.
No one will find it until mowing time
on a hot haymaking day.

The child will not come out of the meadow.
It will die in its flower-bed
in quiet wonder.
Light as a feather it will
finally lie down in
a thicket of vetch
and not think.

Båtane på sanden

Båtane på sanden har dregi seg
saman som til rådsmøte.
Gamle stikk dei snutane i hop
og teier og forstår
(det meste)
som gamle båtar gjer.

Å så lange dei er i kroppen.
Låge og fine på ei strand.
Dei er mørknande i veden
og stillferdig morkne.
Skapte for vatn,
og for å tynast av vatn.
Trekvart er dei uti no òg.
Det dei ikkje veit om væte
veit ingen.

Ingen ting har dei slegi fast
under sitt rådsmøte.
I heile dag har dei legi der urørleg.
Heimkjære båtar.
Fire stykke på ein sand.

The Boats on the Sand

The boats on the sand have drawn together
as if in a council of elders.
They stick their snouts together
and are silent and understand
(most things),
as old boats do.

O, how long their bodies are.
Low and sleek on a beach.
Their wood is darkening
and they are quietly decaying.
Made for water,
and to be destroyed by water.
Even now they're three-quarters in it.
What they don't know about the wet
no one knows.

They haven't settled anything
at their council.
All day they've lain there, motionless.
Boats in the home port they love.
Four of them on a stretch of sand.

Det mørke auget

Det mørke auget
veit ein alltid om.
Det mørke auget kviler
på ein kvar ein er.
Ein er tiltrekt av det.
Det stille auget under
det mørke lauv.

Det liksom sikre auget, fordi det forstår.
Det synest vennleg, og utan grums.
I den stille lund stirer det på ein.
Har si dragkraft ved å vera
uforståeleg.

Stille blad kransar det inn ved kjelda.
Alltid har det vori der.
Det dreg ein, som kjelda dreg,
der ein drakk titt og ofte.

Det er blindt, auget.
Som menneskeauge støypt i malm.
Men i det mørkret og natta kjem,
er det annleis eit sekund.
Blikkar i det.
Slik går det inn i natta
og er borte.

Det gåtefulle umogelege auget
ser på det gåtefulle umogelege
mennesket
—og det skremte mennesket må sjå
tilbake som fuglen på ormen.

Mennesket går oppreist,
men kjenner heile tida auget i ryggen
og må snu seg.

The Dark Eye

You're always aware of
the dark eye.
The dark eye rests
on you wherever you are.
You are attracted by it.
The still eye under
the dark leaves.

The eye that's somehow reliable, because it understands.
It seems friendly, and unclouded.
In the still grove it stares at you.
Casts its spell by being
inscrutable.

Still leaves surround it near the spring.
It has always been there.
It draws you, like the spring
where you've drunk so often.

It is blind, this eye.
Like a human eye cast in iron.
But when the dark and the night come,
it is different for a second.
It stirs.
This is how it enters the night
and is gone.

The mysterious impossible eye
looks at the mysterious impossible
human
—and the frightened human must look back
like a bird at a snake.

People walk upright,
but feel the eye on their backs the whole while
and must turn around.

Tinga kryssar einannan.
Møter og støder einannan.
Riv sund for einannan.
Medan det mørke auget er vitne
frå sin stille lund.

Things intersect.
Meet and support one another.
Or destroy.
While the dark eye observes
from its still grove.

Sky ord

Sei, sei, sei—
Det står i auget.
Det rykker i munnen.
Sei det, sei det.
Det er eit livsens ord
som vil fram,
men ikkje tør.

Vil, vil, vil,
men kan ikkje.
Aldri blir det sagt.
Kvitt slam over det.
Lamme ord døyr på munnen.

Mange mil borte
er kanskje ordet
rispa med redde hender
inn på ein stein.
Der skal det
gjennom tidene
vaskast bort.

Eit ord som ville
slå opp dørene.
Som ville gjera livet annleis.
Som ville, som ville—
Som ikkje kan.

Shy Word

Say, say, say—
It sits in the eye.
It tugs at the mouth.
Say it, say it.
It's a vital word
that wants out,
but doesn't dare.

Wants, wants, wants,
but cannot.
Will never be said.
Covered in white foam.
It dies on the lips.
The paralyzed word.

Many miles away
perhaps the word
is scratched into a stone
by frightened hands.
There, through the ages,
it will be
washed away.

A word that wanted
to open doors.
That wanted to make life different.
That wanted, that wanted—
That cannot.

I underjorda

For hundrende gong
tenker ein uroleg
på dei harde kreka
med skjold på ryggen,
og eit hemmeleg auge
i den evige natt.

Rundslipte gangar
og den evige natt.
Ein snute stikk fram
der ein stein blir oppriven,
men er borte att før nokon
såg kva det var.

Men i raseri blir det
lyst krig mot mennesket,
for den steinens skuld.
Husa deira skal borast opp
til dei sig i hop som mjøl.
Dei vonde auga deira
skal etast rå.

Underworld

For the hundredth time
you think uneasily
of the hard insects
with shields on their backs,
and a secret eye
in the perpetual night.

Burrows polished smooth
and the perpetual night.
A mandible pokes out
where a stone is pried loose,
but is gone again before anyone
can see what it is.

But in fury, war
is declared against humans
on account of that stone.
Their houses shall be drilled through and through
until they collapse like flour.
Their evil eyes
shall be eaten raw.

MARE

om Det Store Sòg

Det store sòget kom som eit lyn, og utan lyd.
Det første bratte berget saugst ned i myrlandet,
rett ned og vart borte.
Det kvarv i myrlandet under høge skrik,
så øyret mitt byrja å brenne.
Det var inga innbilling. Gammal redsle sanna seg.
Nokon i Allheimen gjorde opp sitt mørke bu
og var ferdig.

Auga mine ville vende inn-ut, men eg såg likevel:
Berg etter berg fór same veg.
Sogne ned i det ukjende
under veldige rop.
Etter sitt lange jordeliv
fekk berga i siste stund mæle.
Eg lydde støkt på det, til eg merkte
at øyra mine var falne av, så det vart stilt.
Ropa deira visste eg heretter berre om.

Sjølv var eg ferdig til å falle, men fekk ikkje.
Stivna måtte eg stå og vera vitne.
Berga sokk,
grunnen til det var løynd.
Alt liv som budde i bergskogane
hoppa av i tide, fylte opp i markene,
kravla og krok i tjukke lag på alle kantar,
utan å drepa einannan, som i eit forseint paradis.
Imot meg kom dei òg, som sjøar.
I mi kunstige stille skjøna eg at lufta kokte
av lyd.
Dei kom, men skvatt til side framfor meg,
eller vende om i redsle
—så at det å møte meg måtte vera verre enn alt.

In Thrall:
on The Great Sinking

The great sinking came like lightning, and without sound.
The first steep mountain was sucked down into the marshland,
straight down, and was gone.
It disappeared into the marshes with loud shrieks
so I felt a burning in my ears.
I didn't imagine it. Ancient fears were confirmed.
Someone in the Universe had settled his dark estate
and was finished.

My eyes wanted to turn inside out, but I looked nonetheless:
Mountain after mountain went the same way.
Sucked down into the unknown
with enormous cries.
After their long earthen life
in the end the mountains found a voice.
I listened to it, frightened, till I realized
my ears had fallen off, it was quiet.
After that I only knew their cries must be there.

I expected to fall myself, but I couldn't.
I had to stand there, frozen, and bear witness.
The mountains sank,
the cause was hidden.
All the creatures that lived on the wooded slopes
jumped off in time, filled up the fields,
swarmed and crawled in thick layers everywhere
without killing each other, as if in a latter-day Eden.
They came toward me too, like a sea.
In my peculiar silence I understood that the air was boiling
with sound.
They came, but parted before me,
or turned tail in fear
—as if meeting me must be the worst thing of all.

Egg fekk kjensle av
ei *grueleg skuld.*

Meir trugande og horsk vart vinden
frå dei vide slettene der berga hadde stått.
I synsranda gjekk det siste ned, i vill protest.
Og kva vart det så etterpå:
Som ved trolldom vart det tjukke liv
i myrmarkene borte.
Der rann ikkje ein orm.
Der surra ikkje ei fluge.
Der stod ikkje eit strå.

Då vart dette liksom det verste.
Ingenting forstod eg, anna: bort eg òg.
Det virka til eit sanselaust rop på
huset mitt, huset mitt.
Det ørvesle huset kom lydig farande.
Det hadde stått venta med døra nede ved marka
vidt oppe som eit gap.
Veit ikkje korleis eg kom inn,
men andletet kom inn til sist.
Sjå endå ein gong.
Til døra let seg sjølv i.

I had a sense of
horrible guilt.

The wind from the broad plains
where the mountains had stood grew threatening and raw.
On the horizon the last one went down, wildly protesting.
And what could be found there afterwards?
As if by magic the dense life
in the marshlands was gone.
Not a single snake slithered.
Not a single fly buzzed.
Not a blade of grass remained.

And this was somehow the worst.
I understood nothing, except: I have to flee too.
It became a senseless cry for
my house, my house.
The tiny house came dutifully toward me.
It had stood waiting with its low door
open wide as a chasm.
Don't know how I got inside
but my face came in last.
Had to look one more time.
Until the door closed itself.

Berget som gret
(Eit bilete måla av Sigmund Lystrup)

Berget som gret.
Eit bilete på veggen.
Det flintharde
stupbratte berg.

Ei raud hending skok
steinmassene til det inste.
Berget gret,
og den som laga biletet
måtte gå med dødsbodet
til det unge blod.

Ville bilete dansa for han,
flaut saman frå mange kantar,
der han stod fomla
med blytunge ord.

Slik græt berg.
Slikt krympar hjartet.
Penselen visste det
og leika seg i
eit opent samvet.
Slik vart det diktet om
berget som gret.

Alltid græt berga.
Tusenårs gråt ber dei merke av
når ein kjenner dei.
Berga og gråten
har ein med seg sjølv.

The Mountain That Wept
(A Picture Painted by Sigmund Lystrup)

The mountain that wept.
A picture on the wall.
The flint-hard
steep-cliffed mountain.

A red turn shook
the masses of stone to the core.
The mountain wept,
and the one who would paint the picture
had to take a message of death
to young blood.

Wild images reeled before him,
flowed together from all sides
as he stood fumbling
with leaden words.

That's how mountains weep.
And make the heart cringe.
The paintbrush knew this
and let itself play
with a clear conscience.
That's how it made a poem
of the mountain that wept.

The mountains have always wept.
They bear the marks of a thousand years' weeping
when you know them.
The mountains and the weeping
you carry in yourself.

NOTES

The Norwegian texts in this book are based on those printed in Tarjei Vesaas, *Dikt i samling* (Oslo: Gyldendal, 1972), hereafter cited as *Ds*. A few corrections are noted here; these were undertaken after an examination of the first editions of the individual volumes and consultation with Halldis Moren Vesaas.

Dark Ships Coming / Mørke skip innover—p. 12
In stanza 1, line 4, *Ds* "blågrå" has been corrected to "blygrå."

The Smell of Spring / Vårlukten—p. 22
In stanza 2, line 1, a comma missing in *Ds* has been inserted before the dash.

Dead Lake / Død sjø—p. 33
The image of "drowned shamans" in stanza 4 refers to a well-known episode in *Olav Tryggvasons Saga*, one of the books in Snorre Sturlason's *Heimskringla*, or *The Lives of the Norse Kings*.

Farther and Farther Away / Lenger og lenger bort—pp. 38–39
The dedication refers to the novelist Sigurd Christiansen (1891-1947).

The Glass Wall / Glasveggen—pp. 54–55
Ds omits the stanza break before the fourth stanza; it has been restored here.

Heat / Hete—pp. 78, 80, 82.
In stanza 2, at the end of line 8, a comma faintly visible in the first edition has been restored.
All editions have an extraneous stanza break after line 6 of stanza 3; it has been removed here, as has an errant period after line 10.
In stanza 4, line 8, *Ds* "motrop" has been corrected to "mot-rop."
In stanza 7, line 17, *Ds* "var" has been corrected to "vart."

The Boat / Båten—p. 88
In stanza 1, line 2, *Ds* "for" has been corrected to "fór."

A Nameless Ring in the Wood / Ein namnlaus ring i veden—p. 90
In stanza 1, *Ds* comma at the end of line 4 has been corrected to a period.
Ds inserts an extraneous stanza break after line 3 of stanza 4; it has been removed here.

APPENDIX: A TARJEI VESAAS COLLAGE

> Yes—we are.
> Are simply here
> and are filled by a slow song
> we knew existed
> that no ear has ever heard,
> but that was here before roots took hold
> and before day emerged from its skin.
>
> (From "The Next Pass" [*Lf*])

My birthplace, the farm Vesaas, is an isolated farm in Vinje, Telemark. A good six hundred meters above sea level. On that farm the undersigned was a so-called *odelsgut*[1]—in the tenth recorded generation of *odelsgutar*—so from the outset one was surrounded by a pretty high fence. Wasn't any question what you were going to be when you grew up: ten generations were staring at you. We were three boys, had no sisters. We longed for a sister.

There were a lot of chore-free winter evenings around the paraffin lamp, and quite a few books in the house—as well as the local library to borrow from. Mother and Father loved to read, and taught their sons. Father subscribed to several newspapers. Always at least one from Kristiania [Oslo].

Summers there wasn't much reading. Too tired. Longed for the fall—as upside-down as that may sound.

The girl in *The Great Cycle* whom one worshipped so intensely without saying a word—she was real, and it was a joy and a torment to be in the classroom with her. Naturally one lost her to someone with more initiative.

It never occurred to me to tell Father anything about myself; if I *had* to tell someone, it would be Mother.

In the woods and on the moors something began happening to you after a while: you saw there was a great deal there that was indescribably fine!

[1] Eldest son, expected to take over a farm.

And *it could speak to you.* You could return home filled with such speech, and put away the old hunting gun with a feeling of indifference. This occurred more and more often. Like an intimation that the hunting gun wasn't going to be a friend for life after all. (*Later* it came like a sudden change: guns and hunting became out and out repulsive to me, I never fired another shot.)

Now you walked around in a ferment of shapeless intuitions. It spoke to you.

Then it came to 1914. You were seventeen. You were all ready for a summer of high times, but in August the World War started. News of bloodbaths worse than anyone could have imagined. It burned into you so you could never get it out. The first months you felt like the ground was trembling under your feet—even though it was all happening so far away. Later you got *used* to it—habit protects you and is simultaneously a curse. But you never shook off that war. Not even today. All the horror of the new World War didn't manage to wipe out the memories from 1914. You were seventeen.

In my memory adolescence remains a bitter time. *Except for the books.* The books were a deliverance. The way out was to read. Borrow books from the public library and buy what little you could afford.

Just before New Year 1919 it was off to Kristiania to do military service as a member of the Royal Guards. Seven months. This Kristiania that you knew only from talk and from newspapers.

It probably sounds incredible, but it was a good time. Everything to do with military service, as destructive as it sometimes was—all that meant nothing to me. The only thing that mattered was that I got to go to the theater. To a proper theater. The few crowns I got from home I spent on theater tickets.

You have to consider the first grant for travel abroad as the beginning of a new period for a writer. To get one foot out into the world means an enormous amount. It has some consequences that are obvious—but also others, even more important, that you can't put your finger on right away, but that are just part of your equipment from then on and make themselves felt in hidden ways. Valuable ways, which perhaps you yourself don't discover until a long time afterwards.

Now I craved above all else to be abroad. Now the old dream of the loner's life was entirely abandoned, no more mountain caves and valleys with streams—now it was Europe's great cities with their theaters. First and foremost their theaters. And I held to this so tenaciously that in the nine years from 1925 until my marriage in 1934, I spent more time down in the big cities on the Continent than in Vinje or anywhere else in Norway. I see this as great good fortune. As having the greatest importance for my work. I was more than lucky to be able to arrange things that way.

For years I'd known that I wanted to write a book about *the farm* and the young people who grow up there, about their relationship to the older folks, about the thousand things that are a farm. It *had* to be written sooner or later, by me, given the rather unpleasant situation that had developed for me personally because I had left the farm I was to have taken over. Had to *write* something off my chest. And write a kind of explanation for my own people at home.

Should say something too about the poet who made his debut almost at the last moment, in 1946. The beginnings lay many years back, in my first times together with Halldis Moren. She gave me a volume of selected poems by the unhappy and brilliant Finland-Swedish poet Edith Södergran. There's no way to explain the remarkable effect reading this book had on me. The form of the poems too. It was a disturbing experience, and it aroused a desire to try writing poems—just as all excellent and genuine art inspires you and makes you want to set to work. But nothing came of it, no really serious poems came—no more now than before. They lay gestating somewhere for fourteen years. Then they sprang out again for some unknown reason and became the first attempts at poems in *Kjeldene* [The Springs]. And felt like the most enjoyable things of all to work on.

The unrhymed poems—those were the ones that made me want to try my hand. I felt that in that form I could say more of what I wanted to. All the beautiful poems that I'd read and loved during my entire adult life hadn't had *that* effect. The new form, on the other hand—by the way, to call it a new form is really nonsense, it's as old as the earliest poetry we have. Maybe an old form used in a new way.

The question is how far you can take it. To throw disconnected words across a sheet of paper and let them lie wherever they fall seems to me like a dubious way of writing—but I think it's right that someone should try it out. . . . People should be grateful that there are some who spend precious years of their youth on something that doesn't pay at all, because they have a song inside them. A song can sound terrible, but the song purifies itself, the way a river purifies itself when it floods its banks.

If you write somewhat outside the customary ways, you soon get dangerous labels pinned on you. The worst part of it is that the writer himself doesn't feel the writing is strange or "outside." For example, *I* have been told that I write so that sometimes no one understands a word. As an author I can't get this into my head. That's just great, I think—what's the matter with people! But it's probably the case that the author always imagines an ideal reader who can follow whatever he comes up with.

The reader has to sit down to read without prejudices, so that perhaps he can feel in himself what the writer wanted to get at. One mustn't write so the work can be understood with a cold heart. There ought to be a good deal that the reader only *feels* inside himself. The reader has to have an opportunity to open his hidden spaces.

When I sit down at my desk, I'm prepared to do nothing. You're rested and fresh, you've shaved and washed and eaten a good breakfast, but write—that's plain impossible. And it's in that condition you pass the day, most often—so don't ask me where those thirty or more books have come from. Sit up to my eyes in paper, so full that H. can't breathe when she comes in, sit buried in these endless newspaper clippings about everything imaginable—not to find anything usable, just to have something between my fingers—and that's how the day passes. In the evening when you've started in on the big yawns, you think that just to keep yourself honest you have to write a few words today too, before you go to bed. Nevertheless, you tell schoolchildren that you write because you have a consuming drive to do so—and that's true, too.
  Difficult.

A fib, the whole landscape. But there's surely a *touch* of Telemark in a landscape now and again. Never think about it. It's not that important. You could always arrange yourself a landscape—if that's all a book needed. *(Os)*

I like the modern form. Anyone who absolutely has to *understand* everything he sees misses a lot. It's not always true that "obscure words come from obscure thoughts." *(M)*

This was a *stabbur*[2] once, but it had been made over several times before it became my writing studio. I've made some of the furniture myself—tables and shelves, and a *slagbenk*.[3] The professional carpenters around here say, by the way, that I use far too many nails. *(TV)*

Some valleys in Norway are long and broad and splendid—and maybe Telemark looked like that too one fine morning before it set in its final form, but something must have stirred it all around, and then it set like this, with short, broken-off valleys beyond counting.

In the Telemark terrain there are bound to be many waterfalls. Many of them have been put to good use, but many still go tumbling free. . . . The rivers have been important for this county so rich in forests.

It's wild and tamed and ugly and beautiful by turns in these valleys. Thanks to a great deal of toil we now have a good network of roads, and the view from them certainly isn't boring.

We're landlubbers, and aren't too familiar with the folks who live out on the coast. They send us a truck full of mackerel now and then. And maybe get some planks and brown cheese as payment.

Field and forest have given people their subsistence here. In the valleys each clan lived securely closed off in its own tract. So they kept for a long time what had been passed down to them. They kept alive many fine ballads.

Often you can see cars from all over southern Norway and from several neighboring countries. You cough and get off the through road. There you find centuries-old farms on the hills, side by side. Something permanent. The people there are settled and love their home ground. It makes for sure hands.

[2] Cabin, often on stilts, for storage of food.
[3] Traditional wooden bench, with storage space, that opens to a bed.

Poetry and imagining—yes, there's surely plenty of that around here. But life in these villages is after all a hard struggle for a livelihood—here as elsewhere. It's a good thing people had more *time* some generations back, so they could remember the ballads and get them written down. These days it's as if their hands aren't so caring.

These valleys *were* in any case a home for poetry. Many people whose names we don't know have made songs that will go on living. The poet himself is forgotten and anonymous. He lived in a time when the artist was both proud enough and humble enough not to attach any importance to his name. It was the work that mattered. That's how this priceless treasure was built up, sung poems that no one knows the authors of, but that ever since have been a source to draw on for both new poetry and new music.

Take a man like Vinje[4]—you see him against the background of many anonymous poets in the valleys of Telemark. He was like the fruit of the people's long growth. In him a great legacy was refined in a blaze of spirit and criticism. . . . And now you can't avoid him—just as you can't avoid the high mountains. But I don't mean he blocks your way! On the contrary. He gives you a vantage. And his songs have in them what can't be said in words, something a person always needs, and longs for. *(T)*

What I wanted to do was to tell about the hidden and secret drama that plays itself out in the nighttime, or better, in the gray morning hours, when the new day is breaking over the ridge and every living creature ought to be safe in its home.

A drama that no one gets to witness. *(Fh)*

[4] Aasmund Vinje (1818–70), major Norwegian poet.

SOURCES

A blank line in the collage indicates the omission of one or more paragraphs. The excerpts from each source are not necessarily arranged sequentially according to their order in the respective sources.

Lf: from "Ved neste skar" ("The Next Pass"), in *Lykka for ferdesmenn* (Oslo: Gyldendal, 1949), 93–95.

Os: from Tarjei Vesaas, "Om skrivaren," in *Ei bok om Tarjei Vesaas,* ed. Leif Mæhle (Oslo: Det Norske Samlaget, 1964), 11–33.

M: from Jan Erik Vold, "Møte med Tarjei Vesaas," in *Tarjei Vesaas,* ed. Jan Erik Vold (Oslo: Kulturutvalget i Det Norske Studentersamfund, 1964), rpt. in Vold, *Entusiastiske essays: klippbok 1960–1975* (Oslo: Gyldendal, 1976), 36–42 (the passage quoted is from p. 42).

TV: from "Tarjei Vesaas om seg selv," ed. Brikt Jensen, in *Tarjei Vesaas 1897 – 20. august – 1967,* ed. Edvard Beyer, Bjarte Birkeland, Nils Johan Rud, Tormod Skagestad, Jan Erik Vold (Oslo: Gyldendal, 1967), 85–94. Jensen cites the source of the passage I have quoted (from p. 91) as a television interview conducted by Mette Janson on 12 Dec. 1965.

T: from Tarjei Vesaas, "Telemark," *Kvinnen og Tiden,* 1947, No. 11, 25–29.

Fh: from Tarjei Vesaas, "Fuglar og hus" (1969), rpt. in Tarjei Vesaas, *Huset og fuglen: tekster og bilete 1919–1969,* ed. Walter Baumgartner (Oslo: Gyldendal, 1971), 277–82 (the passage quoted is from p. 278).

INDEX TO NORWEGIAN TITLES

TARJEI VESAAS (1897–1970), the eldest son of a farming family in Telemark, Norway, is among the giants of twentieth-century Scandinavian fiction. He won the Venice Prize in 1952 for a volume of stories, and the Nordic Council Prize in 1963 for the novel *Is-slottet* (*The Ice Palace*). His fiction has been widely translated; eight novels have appeared in English. Starting in 1946, Vesaas published five volumes of poetry during his lifetime; a sixth appeared posthumously in 1970.

ROGER GREENWALD grew up in New York City. His first book of poems, *Connecting Flight*, was published in 1993. In 1994 he won the CBC Radio / *Saturday Night* Literary Award for poetry. His translations of poetry by Rolf Jacobsen, Paal-Helge Haugen, Tarjei Vesaas, and Pia Tafdrup have won awards in the U.S. and Canada. He is the translator and editor of *The Silence Afterwards: Selected Poems of Rolf Jacobsen* (Princeton).

The Silence Afterwards: Selected Poems of Rolf Jacobsen, translated and edited by Roger Greenwald

Rilke: Between Roots, selected poems rendered from the German by Rika Lesser

In the Storm of Roses: Selected Poems by Ingeborg Bachmann, translated, edited, and introduced by Mark Anderson

Birds and Other Relations: Selected Poetry of Dezső Tandori, translated by Bruce Berlind

Brocade River Poems: Selected Works of the Tang Dynasty Courtesan Xue Tao, translated and introduced by Jeanne Larsen

The True Subject: Selected Poems of Faiz Ahmed Faiz, translated by Naomi Lazard

My Name on the Wind: Selected Poems of Diego Valeri, translated by Michael Palma

Aeschylus: The Suppliants, translated by Peter Burian

Foamy Sky: The Major Poems of Miklós Radnóti, selected and translated by Zsuzsanna Ozsváth and Frederick Turner

La Fontaine's Bawdy: Of Libertines, Louts, and Lechers, translated by Norman R. Shapiro

A Child Is Not a Knife: Selected Poems of Göran Sonnevi, translated and edited by Rika Lesser

George Seferis: Collected Poems, Revised Edition, translated, edited and introduced by Edmund Keeley and Philip Sherrard

C. P. Cavafy: Collected Poems, Revised Edition, translated and introduced by Edmund Keeley and Philip Sherrard, and edited by George Savidis

The Late Poems of Meng Chiao, translated and introduced by David Hinton

Selected Poems of Shmuel HaNagid, translated from the Hebrew by Peter Cole

Leopardi: Selected Poems, translated and introduced by Eamon Grennan

The Complete Odes *and* Satires *of Horace*, translated with an introduction and notes by Sidney Alexander

Through Naked Branches: Selected Poems of Tarjei Vesaas, translated and edited by Roger Greenwald